2/23

THE ART OF THE TART

We may live without poetry, music and art;
We may live without conscience, and live without heart;
We may live without friends; we may live without books;
But civilized man cannot live without cooks.

Owen Meredith
(Edward Robert Bulwer, Earl of Lytton)

THE ART OF THE TART

Tamasin Day-Lewis

Photography by David Loftus

CASSELLPAPERBACKS

For Janie
You're my friend —

What a thing friendship is, world without end!
Robert Browning

First published in the United Kingdom in 2000 by Cassell & Co

This paperback edition first published in 2001 by
Cassell Paperbacks, Cassell & Co
Wellington House, 125 Strand
London, WC2R 0BB

A CIP catalogue record for this book is available from the British Library

ISBN 1 84188 132 5

Design Director: David Rowley
Designed by Lucy Holmes
Typesetting by Tiger Typeset
Printed and bound in Italy by Printer Trento S.r.l.

Lemon Tart (page 118)

CONTENTS

"It all starts on a kitchen chair, sleeves rolled,

with a floured, preferably marble surface, and

a wooden rolling pin. The food: the jam tart."

INTRODUCTION

There is a kind of golden age, well before entering the uncharted depths of recipe territory, when you are initiated into a fundamental rite of passage, the cookery lesson. It is the communality of the whole thing, and the complete absorption of all five senses, that make cooking one of the great seminal and sensual experiences of childhood. You watch, you listen, you smell, you copy, you taste, and, according to dexterity, height, strength, the span of attention and of those tiny hands, with the added essential ingredient of greed, the initiation is complete. And this can set you on a course that inspires a love and knowledge of food and cooking, and makes it central to your life.

It all starts on a kitchen chair, sleeves rolled up, with a floured, preferably marble work surface and a wooden rolling pin. The food: the jam tart. Deep in my earliest culinary memory lies the nutty scent of pastry of the prinked-edged tarts, with their bubbling lava-flow of jam struggling to break through the banks and escape the pastry barrier. And the unevenness of their set, your unwillingness to wait, leading to the palate-searing first mouthful, and the jam's scalding deliquescence on to the tongue. The perfect sweet-savoury combination of this tiny, self-contained delicacy that you have helped to make, stretching the pastry until it shrinks back at you like recalcitrant elastic, the plopping and licking of good, fruit-lumped jam from the spoon. That irresistible desire to overfill the tart case: this time it won't burn, it won't overflow... It is as indelible a memory of childhood as puddle jumping, smashing the upturned shell of the egg you've pretended not to eat, the soaring thrill of your first wobbly zigzag on a two wheeler, tying a bow, writing your name.

When I decided to write a book about tarts, I looked back before I looked forwards. Cooking is always about shared memory and experience, and tarts seem to have both fuelled and inspired my passion for food and cooking for longer than I can remember with any reliable degree of honesty and clarity. My memories of jam tarts now are as much about my three children wonkily perched on the afore-mentioned kitchen chair, cuffs hopelessly scuffed with flour in their haste to cut out and roll. The corners of raw pastry are scoffed furtively, clumsy fingers pressing the circles asymmetrically before stickily pushing strawberry, raspberry, bramble and apricot jam off the spoon.

The next step is unquestionably the savoury sophistication of the Quiche Lorraine which, ubiquitous and passé though it may seem to some, is, to my mind, when perfectly executed, with buttery pastry and an unctuously creamy, bacony, barely wobbling interior, infinitely preferable to a would-be-provençale-ingrediented, more fashionable offering. The simple combination of thick, ivory cream, proper oak-smoked bacon, with perhaps a thin veil of Gruyère placed on it, and a butter-dotted top to glisten above a gloriously browned surface – this is food to console and please of the highest order.

Quiche goes well beyond the realms of the domestic science class, though even that has been fatuously excised or sidelined at the exact point in our culinary evolution where the next generation of cooks is confronted with 'heat and eat', partially cooked, ready washed and prepared food that bypasses completely the pleasures of cooking, and is accompanied by the mantra for our times: 'fast food'.

What I want to know about this culinary cul-de-sac that we appear to be going up so willingly, is what are we supposed to be saving this precious time for? And do the television cooks, food manufacturers and supermarkets really believe in this extraordinary marketing campaign that puts speed above taste, skill, creativity, the sense of reward and completeness one feels at having cooked a really good, if simple meal, from start to finish?

The relaxation, pleasure, enjoyment of not just preparing good food, but of eating it in the way in which it is meant to be eaten, savouring it slowly, is all the more important in the current speed-addicted climate in which we live. I find it positively insulting to be told what I haven't got time to do, and then offered a nutritionally suspect and deeply inferior alternative.

Of course there are some foods that are delicious raw, need the minimum of preparation, are divine and quick cooking, or, like a slow-simmered stew, a barely bubbling, somnambulant, stove-top thing, need a perfectly realistic preparation time and can then be left to their own devices. Well, tarts are no different. My pastry is made and rolled in five minutes, and its fridge time varies from nil if I'm really under pressure – I just grate freezer-cold butter into the flour – to several days. Making extra tart cases is eminently possible, as is freezing them. Then it is up to you how long you want to spend making the interior, but – being the simple yet most perfectly self-contained food that it is – it is perfectly possible to achieve in between five and 20 minutes, depending on the complexity of the filling.

The fact that we are being deskilled, that there are actually people frightened of making pastry, or who see it as a kind of Mount Everest in culinary terms, only to be scaled on high days and holidays, mystifies and distresses me.

Anyone reading this book should not doubt their ability to achieve every one of the recipes, and even the least experienced will know at a glance that the more time-consuming ones are not more complicated, the process is merely longer.

If you are going to cheat and dip out of making your own pastry – and, puritan though I am, let me not be accused of being prescriptive – just make sure that it is a superior paste, and that means, for shortcrust or puff pastry, pâte sucrée or pâte sablée, ALL BUTTER. I cannot vouch for these recipes if made with an inferior crust, to my mind there is simply no point. The financial argument is marginal, too; most tarts call for 60g/2oz of butter, which is not going to put you in the bankruptcy courts.

To Jeffrey Steingarten, too, ingredients are non-negotiable. The legendary lawyer-turned-food-critic of American *Vogue*, who the French have honoured with a Chevalier in the Order of Merit for his writing on French gastronomy, and whom I spent a day interviewing in his Manhattan loft for *Food Illustrated*, is unrepentantly firm in his belief that bad cooking is inexcusable. 'Alain Ducasse makes the best tuiles. The recipe is in his book, all you have to do is look it up. Maury Rubin makes the best tart pastry. He has the City Bakery, and he's written a book. His pastry is so tender, so good. It is every baker's obligation to buy the book, or go into a different line of work if his pastry isn't as good.' But here comes the crunch, the get-out clause for those who have attempted a perfectly good recipe, but without the basic wherewithal: 'Technique is the hardest thing to describe. When I wrote my piece on the Ideal American Pie it ran to eight pages. I read every scientific article, and made up a foolproof recipe. It was disgusting. The scientific method didn't work.'

So Jeffrey rang Marion Cunningham, the doyenne of American baking, a 'just beautiful' septuagenarian. 'I asked her to tell me what I'd done wrong. She came and made me a pie, the best pie I've ever had. She talked, I watched. "It's all in the fingers," she said. I couldn't get it all in one, so I rang her and asked her to do it again, five or ten times, over the telephone as I listened and took notes. She was pleading for mercy.'

I am not suggesting this as the prerequisite state of mind for pastry-making, but Jeffrey's inimitable way, that of the obsessive perfectionist, is a similar if not so extreme trait in all the good cooks I know. No amount of scientific reasoning and data can substitute for the methodical care, attention to detail, technique and impeccable ingredients that make soggy or leaden pastry an unlikely event in their kitchens.

I am not so convinced about my reader's unstraying eye or concentration to run to eight pages on the ten-step path to perfection in the construction of fine pastry. I am assuming basic skills and competence, with, perhaps, the added degree of curiosity to at least change the odd habit of a lifetime and try a new method.

My own methods evolve rather than change, and there is very little as satisfying, I find, as cooking something that has been one of your most well used and well loved recipes with a fresh eye and set of instructions. A couple of years ago I turned to Marcella Hazan's ragù recipe, and simply couldn't believe how much better it was than the one I'd thought so brilliant and cooked so often over 20 years.

A lot of the recipes in this book will, I hope, appeal on that level. These are not state-of-the-art, designer dream, fashionable tarts. There are a few recipes that have appeared in cookery books in one guise or another for decades, if not longer. Rather, mine, in some cases, are tweaked, pulled about a bit to reflect my approach to taste, texture, ingredients; everything one cooks makes a statement about oneself, and things like the classic Lemon Meringue Pie, Treacle Tart, Bakewell Tart are hardly cutting-edge cuisine, any more than is the quintessential Quiche Lorraine, but these are tarts that should be remembered, celebrated, reintroduced.

I don't feel that I should have to make excuses or appear cheeky for offering recipes for some of the oldest and best-loved tarts. I remain unmoved on the subject of originality, claiming no more than that the best cooks, like magpies, pick things up along the way; petty thieves if you like, but at least they share the jewels when they discover them!

The great Jane Grigson went into print saying she believed she had created only a few truly original recipes. I admire her high-mindedness, but having learned a seemingly inexhaustible repertoire from her over the years, and on leafing through her, as I regularly do, and still coming across untried recipes, I would rather spurn her notion of originality than agree with her. That way there is also a glimmer of hope for her successors that there is still something worth pursuing in the sharing of their recipes and ways of cooking and eating.

The seasons play such a vital role in my cooking that the recipe testing has, like one of those lingering lunches that just doesn't end, moved imperceptibly through the furred and feathered months, through molluscs and winter roots to soft fruits and shoots, to the pink and greenery of early summer, and the hidden treasures and earthy flavours of the autumn, thanking God, as I perennially do, that there is no closed season for chocolate.

I am not advocating the slavish following of the seasons, nor the xenophobically purist approach of only using indigenous, British-grown and raised foods. By Christmas this year, the sight of a South American raspberry, a Peruvian fig, a South African apricot, followed by the fresh, sharp-scented Seville orange, after months of apples, pears and dried fruits, was irresistible.

I do, however, eat in season, and from locally bred, grown, shot or hooked ingredients most of the time. Without my own deeply inadequate supply of vegetables and herbs, which never fail to thrill when you cut, pull or dig them yourself, augmented by a local box delivery scheme from Merricks Farm at Langport, and fish from Phil Bowditch in Taunton, including local carpet shell clams, Brixham crabs and wild salmon from the Tamar; without the extraordinarily dedicated and inventive Charlotte and Bill Reynolds of Swaddles Green Farm at Buckland St Mary for organic meats and charcuterie, and the nearest – disgracefully – specialist cheese shop, Anne Marie and Tony Down's Fine Cheese Company in Bath, my food and cooking would be altogether less inspired, I would be dramatically less well informed, and my whole pleasure in planning, inventing, cooking and eating would be far less intense.

We need a Fine Cheese Company and a Baker & Spice (see page 141) in every town; not the sempiternal horror of yet more new supermarkets carved into our countryside, further eroding choice and service, and ensuring the hearts of our towns are gutted, filleted, and half emptied of small, original shopkeepers.

Bit by bit one is reduced to the grisly 'speciality counters' of unimaginably dreary, be-clingfilmed slices of unmatured, ill-kempt cheeses; to the dubious advantages of unripenable Third World exotica; and to an erratic stocking and buying policy that left me unable to buy ground almonds, vanilla pods or saffron one week in one of the giants. I will not name and shame. The latter two, I was informed, were too expensive. And yet there was an ill-thought-through section of ludicrously expensive honey with cherries in it, membrillo, dried porcini and Mediterranean olive oils. How much more difficult and expensive to stock all these than, say, for each supermarket to stock the best of their regional suppliers. We have wonderful Devon and Somerset cheeses, local cider, a fantastic eel smoker (Brown & Forrest, at Hambridge), Rocombe Farm ice cream that puts a certain supposedly sexy rival to shame, and fantastic clotted cream.

So what is going on? The food revolution is, not surprisingly, steered but not led by the supermarkets, and it is more in their interest to invent new tubs of ready-made pasta sauce than it is, say, to build a wood-fired bakery like the one at Melmerby in Cumbria and actually show people that the staff of life can also give you the most exciting mouthful you ever tasted. Good bread should provide a culinary framework to all our food, not be a one-off experience for those of us lucky enough to know better, be richer, live closer to the few stalwarts who have struggled to make a go of it.

It's almost funny – but not quite – that such things should be considered aspirational, treats, especially when one remembers that many tiny French villages boast a brace, not just a single boulanger and pâtissier.

I think, without doubt, there was a single defining moment when I realized that there was a complex artistry involved in the highest levels of cooking. Although hitherto unexpected, it had a profound influence, albeit not obvious at the time, on my culinary future. The year, I can't remember, but I had been asked out to dinner by an ex-boyfriend and a wealthy American friend of his, who always espoused good food and female company. It was early days for Pierre Koffmann's Tante Claire, but London was aware that its culinary desert had an oasis in its midst. Royal Hospital Road was not the likeliest of places, concealed soberly and residentially from the thrum and pulse of the King's Road. There, I ate a tart that I can remember visually, and with as close to a taste memory as one can get, that has remained a nonpareil.

A delicate construction of leaf upon leaf of puff pastry, a perfectly poached pear casually gracing its summit, slightly, bitterly caramelized, cloaking, if I am right, a whisper of a crème légère, and served with a Poires William sabayon; Koffmann's Feuilleté aux Poires was a masterpiece – I would give anything for a second helping.

Pretty early on in the conception and testing stages of this book, I realized that it would be inconceivable not to include some of the tarts that friends, cooks and chefs I admire have invented or cooked for me.

Where I've been lucky over the past year has been in being employed to write profiles for *Food Illustrated*'s lovely editor Neale Whitaker. What started as a one-off, we rapidly developed into a series of food-and-life-related conversations with some of the best and most original talent inside the food fraternity. Cooks, chefs, writers, restaurateurs, critics, food historians, arbiters of taste all, I have had an opportunity to talk to and, better still, in some cases to eat with a fascinating, inspiring and generous bunch of people.

It is difficult to meet an ungenerous cook. The very heart of the experience of making food is about sharing, nurture, generosity, the giving of pleasure. When I came to sit down and write, I knew I had to include a section which I think of, provocatively, as Other People's Tarts. I don't distinguish between the accepted great and the good, and those friends of mine who I know to be exceptionally fine home cooks. Prising the recipes off their creators has been an odyssey in itself, not through unwillingness, more for the simple reason that we all of us have more important things to do with our time, though none more so than sitting down to a good dinner. But these recipes, without exception, have constantly led me to the stove excited, curious, analytical, sometimes even hesitantly doubtful if someone revered and respected's recipe seems to need more than fine-tuning, or a recipe that has started its life in a restaurant oven needs a complete conversion job.

The ultimate consolation has been that what started out as no more than a glimmer of an idea has managed to convince me not only that it was worth doing, but also that this most versatile and perfectly self-contained of foods is without doubt one of the great joys of my cooking life, equally as pleasurable in the making as in the eating.

Tamasin Day-Lewis

SAVOURY TARTS

"Cooking is always about shared memory and experience, and tarts seem to have both fuelled and inspired my passion for food and cooking for longer than I can remember."

Potato, Garlic and Parsley Tourte (page 26)

SOUFFLÉD CRAB TART

My local fishmonger, Phil Bowditch, gets his crabs from Brixham, and they sit, freshly boiled and sweetly, saltily juicy, on his counter. I am rarely lazy enough to get him to dress them. I take them home, get a mallet, a hammer and a skewer, and set to work outside on the old mill mounting-block, with bits of shell and flesh flying. It seems extraordinary that in some places, the west of Ireland for one, the bodies are thrown back into the sea, the 'discerning' customers wanting only the white meat of the claws. I use the deliciously rich brown meat as well as the white in this tart, which is spiked with a bit of cayenne and saltily, gooily enhanced with Parmesan and Gruyère. As for the pastry, I think wholemeal flour adds a deliciously complementary texture and nuttiness to the crab. This is one of those sublime dishes, subtle yet strong, airily light yet substantial, that is perfect as a starter, main course, lunch or supper. I have made a lobster version which is equally as splendid, but only in Ireland, where a neighbour's lobster catching is not as stratospherically priced as anywhere else. If you want to try it with lobster do; the rest of the recipe remains as is. A dish to impress and delight equally.

Serves 6
22cm/9 inch shortcrust
   pastry case, chilled
   (page 139)
450g/1lb crab meat, brown
   and white
salt, black pepper, cayenne
3 eggs
1 tbsp each of grated
   Parmesan and Gruyère
250ml/8fl oz double cream
2 tsp French mustard

Preheat the oven to 200°C/400°F/Gas 6. Bake the pastry blind for 10 minutes, then remove the beans, prick the base with a fork, and return to the oven for 5 minutes. Remove the pastry case from the oven and turn the heat down to 190°C/375°F/Gas 5.

Season the crab, going carefully with the cayenne – you want a bit of heat, but nothing overwhelming.

Beat in one whole egg and two yolks, and then the cheeses, cream and mustard. Whisk the two egg whites until stiff, and fold gently and quickly into the mixture. Pour the mixture into the pastry case, and cook for about 30–40 minutes. Check after 30; it should be puffed up but have a slightly wobbly centre, like a soufflé. Remove from the oven and leave to cool for 10 minutes before serving.

A favourite accompaniment is a spoonful of cucumber and avocado sambal: skinned and seeded cucumber and red pepper chopped into tiny dice and mixed with cubes of avocado, lemon juice, olive oil, balsamic vinegar, black pepper and finely chopped dill.

ONION TART

Precisely what the criteria are for a classic tart I cannot say — these things are all subjective — but this, like the Quiche Lorraine, the flamiche, the strawberry tart, is certainly a contender. It is sweetly creamy, the onions softened to death as it were, the flavour gentle yet bold, the textures interlocking perfectly: sandy pastry, soft creaminess, sticky onions.

You can muck about with the filling, adding cheese, chives, sage, thyme, anchovies, sour cream, smoked bacon or what you will, but sometimes simplicity is the strongest suit, and for me, that is as near a definition of a classic as you can get.

A sharply dressed green salad is its ideal companion, and perhaps a glass of chilled rosé.

Serves 6
22cm/9 inch shortcrust
   pastry case, chilled
   (page 139)
100g/3½oz unsalted butter,
   or half butter and half
   olive oil
4 large onions, finely sliced
salt
4 large egg yolks, plus
   beaten egg for brushing
300ml/10fl oz organic
   double cream
black pepper, nutmeg

Leave the pastry case in the fridge while you cook the onions for the filling.

Melt the butter, or butter and olive oil, in a large, heavy-bottomed frying pan and add the onions and a pinch of salt, stirring until the onions are well coated in the butter. Then cover the pan with a lid and cook incredibly gently until the onions are well softened but not coloured. Remove the lid and carry on cooking to evaporate all the liquid, stirring from time to time. This whole process will take somewhere between 40 minutes and 1 hour. Set aside to cool.

Preheat the oven to 190°C/375°F/Gas 5. Bake the pastry blind for 15 minutes, then remove the beans, prick the base with a fork, and return to the oven for a further 5 minutes. Brush beaten egg lightly over the surface and turn the oven down to 180°C/350°F/Gas 4.

Beat the egg yolks with the cream, pepper, and a suspicion of grated nutmeg, and stir into the onions, then pour the mixture into the pastry case. Bake for about 30–40 minutes, until gently set and palely browned. Remove from the oven and leave to cool for at least 10 minutes before serving.

QUICHE LORRAINE

I hesitated, distrusted the strength of my feelings for this dish, until I happened upon Simon Hopkinson's eulogy to it, albeit whilst describing how to make a different tart altogether. I have always consigned fashionability to its rightful place, well behind taste and style and personal preference, but this dish, as I have said in my introduction, has suffered more than most since its 1960's and '70's ubiquity. The downgrading from, as it were, couture to high street, the demands of cheap chic in this case bastardizing both method and ingredients, means that many people have only experienced the ready-to-wear, or in this case ready-to-eat version. And this despite the fact that its few classic ingredients and instructions ensure a creation of such consummate superiority that there is no comparison. Any more than there is between instant coffee and the real thing. So, telling it like it is is imperative.

This dish goes back at least as far as the 16th century. Too bad if at its half millennium it should only be known as it is popularly misapprehended.

Cream, eggs and smoked bacon are the triumvirate, the final result dependent on the quality of this trilogy as much as on the skills of the cook. This is the real McCoy, a classic.

Serves 6
6 rashers of organic smoked streaky bacon
300ml/10fl oz organic double cream, Jersey if you can get it
1 organic egg and 3 yolks
black pepper

Make shortcrust pastry (page 139) with 120g/4oz organic white flour and 60g/2oz unsalted butter, binding the mixture with an egg and a scant 2–3 tablespoons of water. After chilling, line a 20cm/8 inch tart tin and prick the base with a fork. Preheat the oven to 200°C/400°F/Gas 6.

Snip the bacon into strips and cook them gently in a frying pan until the fat begins to run. They should remain pinkly soft, not crispened. Drain, cool slightly, then spread over the bottom of the pastry case. Whisk together the cream, egg, yolks and pepper, then pour into the pastry case and place in the oven for 20 minutes. Turn the heat down to 180°C/350°F/Gas 4 for a further 10–15 minutes, until the filling is goldenly puffed up like a soufflé.

Remove from the oven and leave for 10 minutes before serving. Scalding tarts don't taste of anything.

SOUFFLÉD CHEESE TART

This is really about turning an airy soufflé into something more substantial: strands of gooey Gruyère and salty Parmesan suspended in a glossy, thick béchamel, then elevated to soufflé status with whisked egg white. Simple. A workday supper or something smarter, this is a simply delicious dish. Add a teaspoon of English mustard if you want a bit more heat. You might prefer to make the pastry with wholemeal flour.

Serves 6

22cm/9 inch shortcrust
   pastry case, chilled
   (page 139)
beaten egg, for brushing
150ml/5fl oz milk
2 bay leaves
30g/1oz butter
30g/1oz plain flour
black pepper, cayenne
1 tsp English mustard
   (optional)
60g/2oz Gruyère, grated
30g/1oz Parmesan, grated,
   plus a handful for
   sprinkling
2 eggs, separated
1 tbsp double cream

Preheat the oven to 200°C/400°F/Gas 6. Bake the pastry blind for 20 minutes, then remove the beans, prick the base with a fork, brush with beaten egg, and return to the oven for 5 minutes.

Heat the milk gently with the bay leaves. Make a thick béchamel sauce with the butter, flour and warm milk. Season with pepper, a touch of cayenne, and the mustard if you're using it. Add the Gruyère and Parmesan and remove from the heat. Whisk the egg yolks with the cream and stir them into the sauce. Leave the mixture to cool, then remove the bay leaves and fold in the stiffly beaten egg whites. Pour into the pastry case, sprinkle on a handful of coarsely grated Parmesan, and cook for about 15 minutes, until puffed up, browned, and still slightly trembly. Leave to rest for 10 minutes before serving.

MASCARPONE AND BACON TART

Perfect for a leftover, day-before-shopping sort of supper, when the fridge and the storecupboard are contending for most empty space and inspiration is consequently at a low ebb, and subservient to a dearth of ingredients to choose from. I derive a sort of perverse satisfaction from this state of affairs, feel as spoilt by lack of choice as I do from excess of it, for, far from being an inhibitor of the imagination, it is the master of it. Call it 'Empty Fridge Tart' if you like, and if you've no bacon, prosciutto or scraps of gammon clinging to a bone, I can only suggest you go next door and borrow some, or turn to the herb tart recipe (page 51) and adapt it according to the state of your garden, your fridge and the time of year.

Mascarpone or full fat cream cheese work well in this plainly delicious and easy tart. Sieving the cheese before you beat it into the cream and eggs ensures a beautifully smooth result.

Serves 6

6 rashers of smoked streaky
    bacon or pancetta
200g/7oz mascarpone
    or full fat cream cheese
a generous 150ml/5fl oz
    double cream
1 egg and 3 egg yolks
black pepper

Make shortcrust pastry (page 139) with 120g/4oz organic white flour and 60g/2oz unsalted butter, binding the mixture with an egg and a scant 2–3 tablespoons of water. Chill, then line a 22cm/9 inch tart tin and prick the base with a fork. Preheat the oven to 200°C/400°F/Gas 6.

Cut the bacon or pancetta into 1cm/½ inch strips and fry gently until the fat runs. Cool slightly, then spread over the bottom of the pastry case. Whisk everything else together until thick and creamily smooth, and pour into the pastry case. If the cheese is really thick you can add a tablespoon or two of Jersey milk to it. Cook for 20 minutes, then turn the oven down to 180°C/350°F/Gas 4 and cook for a further 10–15 minutes, until golden brown and well risen. Remove from the oven and leave to rest for 10 minutes before turning out and serving.

TOMATO AND PROSCIUTTO TARTS

I seem to have temporarily forsaken the notion of serving a starter — most of the time.
Nothing delights me more in a good restaurant, but at home there seems to be a long overdue,
silent but militant consensus that when cooking for friends, we cooks want to talk to them too.
The days of dinner parties where one bobs like a cork from kitchen to drawing room, missing
punchlines and the threads of all the good conversations until the food has been cleared away,
are a thing of the past. Aside from which, the protein overkill of having both meat and fish,
or the sensation of being awash with soup before one starts the main course, are not something
I want to feel de rigueur about. Particularly on a weekday, when a single good cheese or
perhaps a glass of vin santo with cantucci to dip into it is the perfect way to end a meal.

These tarts, assembled before everyone arrives, are perfect as an ambulant starter.
You can whisk them into and out of the oven, and hand them round while people drink,
without missing a beat. If you can't find good plum tomatoes, use halved organic cherry
tomatoes instead.

I made a large version for an early summer lunch with 300g / 10oz puff pastry rolled out
to about 30cm / 12 inches square, that just fitted my large baking sheet, and it fed six.

Makes 8 small tarts
8 slices of prosciutto,
   San Daniele if possible
150ml/5fl oz best virgin
   olive oil
3 cloves of garlic
black pepper
10 plum tomatoes, or about
   40 cherry tomatoes
a handful of basil, and the
   same of either thyme
   or rosemary

Preheat the oven to 190°C/375°F/Gas 5. Start with 300g/10oz of pure butter puff pastry (see page 141); this tart is characterized by its buttery, oily flakiness. Roll it out and stamp it into eight 10cm/4 inch circles, then place them on a greased baking sheet and leave them in the fridge until you need them.

Tear the prosciutto roughly and put it in the food processor with half the olive oil, the garlic cloves and the pepper. Blitz for a few seconds to make a rough purée.

Slice the plum tomatoes, or halve if you are using the cherry ones. Tear the basil leaves and add them to the remaining olive oil, but not more than 20 minutes before you are going to use them or they will bruise and blacken.

Spoon a mound of the prosciutto mixture on to each tart base, leaving a good-sized clear edge. Place a circle of tomatoes on top, brush with a little of the oil and basil mixture, sprinkle with roughly chopped thyme or rosemary, and cook for about 15 minutes, until the pastry is puffed up and cooked through. Put the tarts on a rack and brush with the oil and basil mixture, then serve warm.

LEEK, POTATO AND OATMEAL TART

Leeks and oatmeal are as much a part of Ireland's culinary heritage as praties. So I decided to combine this trinity in a tart, a wintery, substantial dish, that needs nothing more than a gutsy provençale tomato salad served alongside it.

Serves 6
30g/1oz butter
the whites of 4 thick leeks, sliced 3mm/⅛ inch thick
1 clove of garlic, finely chopped
salt and black pepper
1 egg and 1 egg yolk
150ml/5fl oz single cream
nutmeg
60g/2oz good, mature Cheddar (Montgomery if possible), grated
60g/2oz Parmesan, grated
3–4 medium potatoes, peeled and boiled until just tender, then finely sliced
1 tbsp fresh thyme leaves

Make your shortcrust pastry in the normal way (page 139), but use 60g/2oz flour, 60g/2oz rolled oats and 60g/2oz butter. Chill, then roll out and line a 22cm/9 inch tart tin and return the tin to the fridge for at least 30 minutes. Preheat the oven to 190°C/375°F/Gas 5. Bake the pastry blind for 10 minutes, then remove the beans and return the tart case to the oven for 5 minutes.

Heat the butter in a frying pan and sauté the leeks and garlic gently until softened, then season them. Whisk together the egg, yolk and cream, and season with salt, pepper and a suspicion of grated nutmeg. Mix together the Cheddar and Parmesan.

Spread the leek mixture over the pastry base, add a layer of potatoes, half the thyme, more seasoning, and half the mixed cheeses, then add a second layer of potato. Pour over the cream and egg mixture, and scatter over the rest of the cheese and thyme. Return to the oven for about 25 minutes, until the top is deliciously browned. Allow to cool briefly before serving.

FENNEL, TALEGGIO AND CARDAMOM TART

This is one of those tarts that started off as a complete disaster. In my mind, the mild, subtle aniseed of Florentine fennel combined with sweet baked garlic and sharp, salty goats' cheese. I steamed and puréed the fennel, baked a head of garlic and popped out the cloves like teeth out of their sockets and, with a savoury custard, added the crumbled cheese to the purée. The delicate, pistachio green looked a picture, but the fennel had disappeared, overwhelmed, and the texture didn't have the requisite bite for me.

So I started all over again. This time I chose cardamom as an unobvious but possibly marriageable partner. Susan, my editor, suggested playing down the cheese and using Taleggio. The cardamom did just what it was told to do, it scented without overwhelming; the fennel took the front row, and my brother Daniel and his wife Rebecca were the guinea pigs for a late, light Monday lunch. We were all delighted with the result, which we demolished with a watercress and red chard salad dressed with walnut oil, olive oil and cider vinegar.

Serves 6
22cm/9 inch shortcrust
   pastry case, chilled
   (page 139)
4 bulbs fennel
30g/1oz butter
4 tbsp each of olive oil, white
   wine and water
the crushed seeds of
   8 cardamom pods
2 heaped tbsp crème fraîche
2 eggs and 2 egg yolks
250ml/8fl oz double cream
about 250ml/8fl oz Jersey
   milk
salt and black pepper
90g/3oz Taleggio

Preheat the oven to 190°C/375°F Gas 5. Bake the pastry blind for 15 minutes, then remove the beans, prick the base with a fork, and return to the oven for 5 minutes.

Remove all the tough outer layers of the fennel, then quarter the bulbs and slice thickly. Put the fennel into a heavy-bottomed frying pan with the butter, olive oil, wine, water and cardamom seeds. Bring to a bubble, reduce to a simmer, cover with a lid and cook gently until the fennel is no longer resistant even at the core. Remove it with a slotted spoon, reserve, and bubble the juices until stickily reduced and syrupy, about 2–3 tablespoons.

Whisk together the crème fraîche, eggs and yolks with enough cream and milk to bring a jugful of the savoury custard to almost 600ml/20 fl oz. Add the fennel liquor to the custard mixture and whisk together thoroughly. Season.

Cube the Taleggio into small squares. Spread the fennel over the pastry base, then scatter the Taleggio over it. Pour on the custard and bake until barely set and browned, about 25 minutes. Eat warm.

POTATO, GARLIC AND PARSLEY TOURTE

Strictly speaking, a tourte is not a tart, but since some tarts have a double crust, and since this is irresistibly delicious, it demands to be included.

Before you decide not to make it because you can't be bothered to make puff pastry, let me tell you what I did last week. I rang Baker & Spice (see page 141) in London (020 7589 4734) and put in an order. For £16 you can buy 1kg of puff pastry, all butter, and your tourte is half-way there. Now, given that that is enough for four tarts, or a tourte and two large tarts, and that you won't have to spend a morning rolling and turning and folding and cursing, this seems like great value, and a corner that you can legitimately cut. I don't live round the corner, but I do carry my tray-sized flat parcel of pastry home to Somerset on the back seat of the car when I get the urge.

Puffed up and golden, with a flood of garlic-scented cream bubbling under its lid, this is a refined but hearty winter dish served on its own, but on Sunday I decided to accompany it with tarragon roast chicken, roast parsnips and carrots Vichy. I cooked it as I do my tatins, in a Le Creuset frying pan, the kind with a short, enamelled ovenproof handle.

Serves 6 – 8
400g/14oz puff pastry
   (page 141)
500g/just over 1lb potatoes,
   sliced very finely
3 cloves of garlic, finely
   chopped
3 tbsp finely chopped
   flat-leaf parsley
salt, black pepper, nutmeg
1 beaten egg and 2 egg yolks
250ml/8fl oz organic double
   cream

Preheat the oven to 200°C/400°F/Gas 6. Roll out two circles of pastry, one slightly larger than the other. Grease your frying pan or gratin dish and line with the larger pastry circle.

In a large bowl, mix the potatoes – which must be sliced very finely, or they will not cook through before the pastry is perfect – together with the garlic, parsley and seasoning. Layer the potatoes into your frying pan or dish, then cover with the pastry lid, sealing the edges with a fork and brushing the top with beaten egg. Cut a cross in the middle of the lid for the steam to escape, and bake for 50 minutes.

Whisk the egg yolks and cream together, remove the pie from the oven and, with a tiny funnel held in the steam-hole, pour in the eggy cream. Please pour slowly, or you'll get a geyser of cream that will then lie on top of your pastry. I know, it happened to me first time round, and with a larger funnel! If you would rather, you can delicately run the tip of a knife blade around the pastry and gently lever the lid up to pour in the cream.

Return to the oven for 10 minutes, then serve the flaky triangular wedges hot from the pan.

Tomato, Goats' Camembert and Herb Tart

This is an utterly compulsive late spring/early summer tart, when the herbs in my garden are flowering and as intensely flavoured as the goats' Camembert. The cheese is melting, yet doesn't surrender its shape, and the strong counterbalance of the Gruyère and the mustard take this tart well out of the orbit of the ordinary. I would serve it any time, any place, anywhere; it oozes rustic sophistication, and is utterly unlike the eggy, creamy dishes we think of when we think of savoury tarts. If you have got time, make your herbed brushing oil the night before, so that the flavours have time to marry.

**Serves 6 for supper,
8 for lunch**

1 tbsp Dijon mustard

100g/generous 3oz Gruyère,
    grated

1 dozen or so organic
    tomatoes, sliced

4 x 125g/4½oz Camembert-
    style goats' cheeses
    (I use Soignon, from
    Sainsbury's), sliced

Herbed brushing oil

125ml/4fl oz extra virgin
    olive oil

1 dsp each of finely chopped
    rosemary, thyme, basil,
    fennel and flat-leaf parsley

1 clove of garlic, crushed

salt and black pepper

1 bay leaf

Combine all the ingredients for the brushing oil in a jar or bowl and leave overnight if possible, or at least for a couple of hours.

Make shortcrust pastry (page 139) with 180g/6oz organic white flour and 80g/2¾oz unsalted butter, but use your best olive oil instead of water – you might need a bit more than 2 tablespoons. Chill, then roll out and line a 30cm/12 inch tart tin.

Preheat the oven to 190°C/375°F/Gas 5 and put a baking sheet in the oven.

Spread the mustard over the pastry base, then scatter over the Gruyère. Cover with alternate overlapping slices of tomato and goats' cheese in concentric circles, then brush two-thirds of the herby oil over the surface. Bake the tart on the preheated baking sheet for about 35 minutes; it will be heaving, brown and bubbling. Remove from the oven, brush with the remaining oil, and leave to cool for at least 10 minutes before turning out and serving.

A broad bean and asparagus salad would dress it up, a simple green one would dress it down.

FLAMICHE

A classic northern French tart, which can also be made with the galette yeast dough (see page 104), or covered with a second tier of pastry and turned into a more substantial pie. The scent of leeks sweating gently, sweetly, in butter is one of the great kitchen smells, subsiding as they do into a collective mess that is all buttery white purée. The addition of ham, bacon, pancetta, whilst fine if that is what you feel like, takes away from the purity of the flamiche, which is all about leeks, butter and cream. Full stop! Use only the firm, inner white core of the leeks. Keep your colour for the side, say some of the new leaves that are on the market now — red chard, mustard, tat soi, pak choi — with a grainy mustard dressing to instil a sharp note.

Serves 6
22cm/9 inch shortcrust
   pastry case, chilled
   (page 139)
1.35kg/3lb leeks
about 90g/3oz unsalted
   butter
150–300ml/5–10fl oz
   organic double cream
3 egg yolks
salt, black pepper, nutmeg

This tart is not baked blind, so allow time for your leeks to cool before spreading the wilted, white heap on the pastry.

Trim off the coarse, green outer leaves of the leeks and chop the white parts into roughly 1cm/½ inch rings. Sweat them slowly in the butter, and when thoroughly softened leave them to cool.

Preheat the oven to 180°C/350°F/Gas 4. The amount of cream you use will depend on your tart tin: a shallow tin will be fine with the smaller amount, but you will need more to fill a deeper sided tin. Whisk together the cream and egg yolks, and season with salt, pepper and a suspicion of grated nutmeg. Stir this into the leeks, and spread the mixture quickly and evenly over the pastry base. Cook for 35–40 minutes, until tremblingly set. Leave for 10 minutes before turning out and serving. I think this is good cold, too, on a picnic, although if you gauge it right and wrap it up tightly in foil it is perfection, barely tepid, on a cold, Irish beach.

CHARD, GRUYÈRE AND CRÈME FRAÎCHE TART

Swiss chard has a kind of mild, crunchy earthiness which needs gentle enhancing rather than masking, but it adds good texture and flavour and has the virtue of being somehow unexpected.

I found some wonderfully squat bunches with thick, wide, flat white ribs and racing green, shiny, squeaky leaves in a lovely shop called Dandelion on the Wandsworth / Clapham border. My great friend Janie and I had been tramping across the common on a particularly grisly, drizzly March day, on a quest for some good soup and vegetables for a late lunch. Dandelion provided both, and I decided that gooey-sharp Gruyère, crème fraîche and the blanched white ribs of chard would make a delicious tart. Back in Somerset, this is what I did:

Serves 6
22cm/9 inch shortcrust
    pastry case, chilled
    (page 139)
2 heads of Swiss chard
beaten egg, for brushing
200ml/7fl oz crème fraîche
    (I used the delicious
    organic Rachel's Dairy one)
4–6 tbsp Jersey milk
1 egg and 4 egg yolks
100g/generous 3oz Gruyère,
    grated
¼ tsp cayenne
salt and black pepper

Preheat the oven to 200°C/400°F/Gas 6.

Strip the leaves off the chard, and wash the leaves and ribs carefully. Then slice the ribs rather like you would celery, to about 1cm/½ inch widthways, and steam them until tender. Drain and leave to cool.

Bake the pastry blind for 15 minutes, then remove the beans, prick the base with a fork, brush with beaten egg, and return to the oven for 5 minutes. Turn the oven down to 180°C/350°F/Gas 4.

Beat the crème fraîche, milk, egg and yolks together until smooth, then stir in the cheese and cayenne, and, sparingly, some salt and pepper.

Quickly assemble a layer of cooled chard ribs on the pastry base, pour over the custard, and cook until browned, about 30 minutes. I served mine with the steamed chard leaves with a spritz of lemon and black pepper, and some gingery glazed carrots.

SORREL TART

The lemony-sharp flavour of sorrel in a soup or a hollandaise sauce is always a foil to the richness of eggs, cream, butter. It is also less frequented territory than the ubiquitous spinach that people usually grow alongside it. A row of its yellowy-green leaves, shooting up like weeds, is all you need, but if you don't grow it, good supermarkets like Waitrose stock it regularly, albeit in dolls' sized plastic envelopes. Its tartness here, reminiscent of the astringence of rhubarb, with which it shares the constituent oxalic acid, is assuaged by the sweetness of the onions.

Serves 6
22cm/9 inch shortcrust
   pastry case, chilled
   (page 139)
beaten egg, for brushing
300g/10oz sorrel,
   washed and stemmed
60g/2oz unsalted butter
300g/10oz onions, finely
   sliced
2 eggs and 2 egg yolks
325ml/12fl oz organic
   double cream
salt and black pepper

Preheat the oven to 190°C/375°F/Gas 5. Bake the pastry blind for 15 minutes, then remove the beans, prick the pastry all over with a fork, and return to the oven for a further 5 minutes. Remove from the oven and brush with beaten egg.

Throw the sorrel into a saucepan full of boiling salted water, and take it out and drain it the moment it comes back up to the boil. The leaves will be an unappetizing greyish colour, but don't let that put you off. Stew them in 30g/1oz of the butter until all their liquid has evaporated, and they have wilted down into a purée; this will take about 20 minutes. Do likewise with the onions, which will take a bit longer, keeping them covered, and occasionally giving them a stir. They should not brown, but be meltingly translucent, a pale tangle.

Mix the onions with the sorrel in a bowl and leave until tepid. Whisk the eggs and yolks with the cream and seasoning and stir into the sorrel mixture. Pour into the pastry case and cook for about 35–40 minutes, until barely set and barely coloured. Leave to cool for at least 10 minutes before turning out and serving.

CEP AND RED ONION TART

This is a wonderfully intense, musky-flavoured tart, perfect for the lean, wintery months when one turns more to the storecupboard and to dried foods than at any other time of year. The mascarpone, delicately enhanced by the cep liquor, makes it less rich than if it was full of cream, and it doesn't set in quite the same way as the eggier tarts; it rather slides slowly off its pastry base when sliced, like an earthy, densely flavoured ragout. This makes an exquisite and original starter.

Serves 10 as a starter
6 as a main course
60g/2oz dried ceps
2 medium-sized red onions
30g/1oz unsalted butter
250g/9 oz mascarpone
1 large egg and 3 egg yolks
8–10 sage leaves, or the
    leaves from 2–3 sprigs
    of thyme
salt and black pepper

Soak the ceps in 300ml/10fl oz of warm water for about an hour, turning them when you remember, to ensure they're all completely rehydrated.

Meanwhile, make shortcrust pastry (page 139) with 120g/4oz wholemeal or organic white flour – a wholemeal crust is always delicious with fungi. Chill, then roll out and line a 22cm/9 inch tart tin – or a rectangular tin measuring 35 x 12cm/14 x 5 inches. Preheat the oven to 200°C/400°F/Gas 6. Bake the pastry blind for 10 minutes, then remove the beans, prick the base with a fork, and return to the oven for 5 minutes. Remove from the oven and brush the pastry with a little beaten egg. Turn the oven down to 180°C/350°F/Gas 4.

Strain the ceps, pressing gently, and reserve the liquid. Slice the onions finely into rings, and sweat them gently in the butter for a few minutes until they're softened. Chop the ceps coarsely, add them to the onions and cook for a further few minutes. Strain the cep liquid into the pan and let it reduce completely, then tip the mixture into a bowl and leave until it is cold. You can complete the cooking to this stage several hours before if it is more convenient.

Whisk the mascarpone, egg and yolks together, then add the finely chopped sage or thyme and stir in the cep and onion mixture. Season, then spread the mixture over the bottom of the pastry case and cook for 10 minutes. Turn the heat down to 160°C/325°F/Gas 3 and cook for a further 25–30 minutes. Check after 25, to see quite how unfirm it is. Remove from the oven, still obviously shuddery, and leave for 10 minutes before turning it out and eating it warm.

L'ALIGOT TART

I write this in some trepidation. I know for sure it will not meet with the approval of Simon Hopkinson, although it is a rare occasion when he doesn't see eye to eye with Elizabeth David. In her classic French Provincial Cooking, *Elizabeth David writes about* l'aligot, *a country dish that she came across at Entraygues, 'a little town on the confluence of two rivers, the Lot and the Truyère, in south-western France.' Floury potatoes, butter, cream, salt and garlic, and tomme de Cantal, a soft, white unfermented local cheese, are the ingredients, but Mrs David suggests that in the absence of tomme de Cantal, which is not a great traveller, and should not be eaten when more than three or four days old, one can substitute the mild, easily melting Caerphilly, or an unmatured Lancashire — of which a little less, as it is stronger flavoured. Simon Hopkinson is adamant: 'I strongly disagree.' He travels to Michel Bras' restaurant in Laguiole in the Auvergne, and enjoys his authentic* l'aligot *as part of a two-starred lunch.*

Well, I still haven't experienced the real thing, but I know of the affinity between potatoes, garlic and cheese, and I can promise you that a combination of the most melting of Italian cheeses, Fontina, and crumbled Caerphilly makes a delicious and robustly filling tart.

Make a larger-than-you-need quantity of the filling, and you can turn the remainder into potato cakes, flouring them lightly and frying them in butter until crustily bronzed.

Serves 6

22cm/9 inch shortcrust
   pastry case, chilled
   (page 139)
beaten egg, for brushing
1kg/about 2lb floury potatoes
salt and black pepper
150ml/5fl oz single cream
60g/2oz unsalted butter
1 clove of garlic, crushed
150g/5oz each of Fontina
   and Caerphilly, cut into
   small dice

Preheat the oven to 200°C/400°F/Gas 6. Bake the pastry blind for 20 minutes, then remove the beans, prick the pastry with a fork, brush with beaten egg and return to the oven for 5 minutes.

Meanwhile, cook the potatoes in their skins, then peel them and mash them thoroughly with some salt and pepper. Heat the cream and butter together in a saucepan, then mix with the mashed potatoes, stirring vigorously with a wooden spoon. Add the garlic and the diced cheeses, and stir until well amalgamated.

Turn the oven down to 160°C/325°F/Gas 3. Fill the pastry case with the potato mixture, and cook the tart for about 20 minutes. Leave to cool for 10 minutes before turning out and serving.

SMOKED BACON AND GARLIC TART

Sweet, soft heads of garlic, oiled, wrapped and baked in their skins, are a delicious contrast to the fat, smoky strips of juicy bacon, these two heavier notes lifted by the fresh taste and verdant colour of chopped parsley. Do not blench at the garlic: blanch. The quantity of garlic might imply dragon's breath, but the blanching — in this case the virtual steaming of the little buds sealed like bodies in a sauna — ameliorates, sweetens, makes mild of this ferocious bulb. Even more so when the new season's garlic comes in.

Virgil said that garlic is the right food to maintain the strength of harvest reapers. I don't think the modern equivalent would complain of lack of substance if confronted by this dish.

Serves 6

22cm/9 inch shortcrust
    pastry case, chilled
    (page 139)
beaten egg, for brushing
3 heads of garlic
3 tbsp olive oil
3 rashers of oak-smoked
    organic bacon, or about
    90g/3oz of cooked,
    smoked gammon
butter for frying, if using
    gammon
2 tbsp chopped flat-leaf
    parsley
1 egg and 2 egg yolks
100ml/3½fl oz each of
    double cream and
    Jersey milk

Preheat the oven to 200°C/400°F/Gas 6. Bake the pastry blind for 15 minutes, then remove the beans, prick the base with a fork, brush with beaten egg, and return to the oven for 5 minutes.

Put each head of garlic on a square of foil big enough to scrunch up tightly and seal it in, dribbling a spoonful of olive oil over each head before you wrap it up. Put the garlic in a roasting tin and bake until soft. Test with a skewer after 25 minutes.

Snip the bacon into strips and cook gently in a frying pan until the fat runs. If using cooked gammon, fry it in a little butter. Off the heat, throw in the parsley and stir until it is coated in the bacon fat. Unwrap the garlic and pop the buds out on to a plate.

Whisk together the egg, yolks, cream and milk. Put the garlic, bacon and parsley into the bottom of the pastry case, then pour in the custard and bake for about 25 minutes. Remove from the oven and leave for about 10 minutes before turning out and serving.

MONKFISH TART WITH BÉARNAISE

*Serves 6 as a main course,
or makes 10–12 small tarts*
22cm/9 inch shortcrust
    pastry case, or 10–12
    small tart cases, chilled
    (page 139)
beaten egg, for brushing
500g/about 1lb monkfish,
    skinned and sliced
salt and black pepper
butter
375g/12–14oz chanterelles
    or organic mushrooms,
    cleaned and chopped
a handful of tarragon

Béarnaise sauce
2 tbsp tarragon vinegar
1 shallot, finely chopped
3 tsp finely chopped tarragon
150g/5oz unsalted butter
2 egg yolks

This can be made either as one whole tart, or as little tarts that just need a last-minute assembly job before serving with drinks — an ambulant starter. They only need 5 minutes in the oven, and everything can be prepared in advance. Monkfish is tenderly, juicily fleshy, so there is no chance of the tarts drying out. If you can get hold of wild mushrooms for the base, do, chanterelles particularly; if not, some organic mushrooms will do fine.

Preheat the oven to 200°C/400°F/Gas 6. Bake the pastry blind for 20 minutes if it is a large tart, 10 minutes if small, then remove the beans, prick the base with a fork and brush with beaten egg before returning to the oven, for 10 or 5 minutes respectively. The pastry should be crisp and cooked. Turn the heat up to 220°C/425°F/Gas 7.

Season the slices of fish and fry them in a generous chunk of butter on both sides, until just opaque. Remove the fish from the pan and add the mushrooms, cooking them until they are completely softened.

Make the béarnaise by heating together the tarragon vinegar, shallot and 1 teaspoon of the chopped tarragon in a small stainless steel saucepan, until the liquid has almost all evaporated. Melt the butter in a small saucepan and leave to settle for a minute or two. Remove the vinegar mixture from the heat, add the egg yolks and whisk until thick. Then, little by little, very slowly pour in the hot melted butter, leaving behind the white residue, whisking as you go. Sieve the sauce and scatter in another 2 teaspoons of chopped tarragon.

Put the mushrooms in the pastry case, followed by the slices of monkfish, then pour over the béarnaise. Sprinkle on a bit more tarragon, and put the tart or tarts in the oven for a quick blast of heat: 5 minutes is all they need. Serve at once.

BRANDADE TART

I first ate brandade de morue in Provence, unsurprisingly, where it is something of a national dish. The morning markets in the glorious towns of Apt, Cavaillon, Carpentras and l'Isle-sur-la-Sorgue, where the summer heat filters down through huge plane trees and all life is brighter, slower, more headily scented, are the places to buy it. Huge, dirty, cream triangles are hung out to dry like old, bald sheepskin rugs, their curious fishy salt smell hanging in the air; you point, you insist on a piece from the middle, not the tail — the bottom handkerchief corner is more salt, less succulence — and then you take it home and launder it like sheets, in several changes of water, for a good 24 hours.

Classically, it is accompanied by bread fried in olive oil and strong black olives. This is a dish the southern French traditionally serve on religious festival days, at Easter and Christmas, but it is great all the year round, and translates well into tart format. Make sure you use your best olive oil.

Serves 6 as a main course or makes 10–12 small tarts
22cm/9 inch shortcrust pastry case, or 10–12 small tart cases, chilled (page 139)
beaten egg, for brushing
1 large potato, about 150g/5oz, peeled
450g/1lb chunk of salt cod, soaked in several changes of water for at least 24 hours, then drained
150–300ml/5–10fl oz cold pressed olive oil
150–300ml/5–10fl oz creamy milk
3 cloves of garlic
1 lemon
black pepper
Provençal black olives and flat-leaf parsley

Prebake your tart case or cases completely for this dish as for the Monkfish Tart on page 39; then turn the heat up to 220°C/425°F/Gas 7.

Steam the potato in chunks until cooked, then mash it or put it through the coarse blade of a mouli-légumes.

Run your fingers over the soaked cod and use tweezers to pull out any bones. Either put the fish in a saucepan of cold water, bring to the boil, switch off instantly and leave for a few minutes, or pour boiling water over it to cover and leave for 10–15 minutes, until a fork can flake it without resistance.

Warm the olive oil in a saucepan and do likewise with the milk and garlic in another pan. Skin the cod and put it in chunks into a food processor, switch on, and pour in the olive oil and milk alternately, in a slow, steady stream. You can either add or discard the garlic. When you have a thick paste, turn it into a bowl and stir in the mashed potato with a wooden spoon. Add the juice of up to the whole lemon, to taste, and black pepper. You won't need salt. Turn into the pastry case or cases, return to the oven for 5 minutes, then decorate with the olives and parsley, and serve warm.

SCALLOP, ARTICHOKE AND SMOKED BACON TART

January. The leanest month. But there are fat, sweet scallops and earthily misshapen Jerusalem artichokes, twisted knobbly roots that are a peeler's nightmare, but worth every knuckle-grating minute. This combination, a dark-dayed inspiration, is one I would even go so far as to say I was proud of and, unusually, it was perfect first time round. A seriously special tart.

Serves 6 – 8

22cm/9 inch shortcrust
    pastry case, chilled
    (page 139)
180g/6oz Jerusalem
    artichokes
6 large scallops, cleaned,
    with the whites separated
    from the corals
4 rashers of smoked
    streaky bacon
300ml/10fl oz
    double cream
3 tbsp Jersey milk
2 eggs and 2 egg yolks
salt and black pepper

Leave the pastry case in the fridge while you prepare the filling. Preheat the oven to 190°C/375°F/Gas 5.

Peel the artichokes and slice them into thin coins, 3mm/⅛ inch thick. Steam until tender, then leave to cool. Slice the whites of the scallops into three discs each, and the corals into two if they are bumper sized. Snip the bacon into thin pieces and fry in its own fat until really crispy. Drain and dry on kitchen paper.

Line the pastry base with the cooled artichokes, then cover with a layer of the raw scallops, distributing them evenly, then dot with the bacon.

Whisk the cream, milk, eggs and yolks together, season, and, using a jug, pour gently into the pastry case so as not to displace the filling ingredients. Cook for 35 – 40 minutes; the corals will stick out of the top in their deliciously gaudy-coloured way, and be just cooked. Leave to cool for 10 minutes, then turn out and serve with a mustardy dressed plain green salad.

SMOKED HADDOCK AND WATERCRESS TART

Watercress is every bit as much a player as spinach with smoked haddock, the iron-rich peppery leaves cutting the sweet smokiness. This is a wonderful everyday tart loved by everyone in my family.

Serves 6
22cm/9 inch shortcrust
    pastry case, chilled
    (page 139)
beaten egg, for brushing
325g/12oz undyed smoked
    haddock
300ml/10fl oz Jersey milk
30g/1oz butter
1 small onion, finely chopped
1 stick of celery, finely
    chopped
30g/1oz plain flour
salt, black pepper, nutmeg
a bunch of watercress
    (stalks removed),
    finely chopped
2 eggs, beaten
2 tbsp grated Parmesan

Preheat the oven to 190°C/375°F/Gas 5. Bake the pastry blind for 10 minutes, then remove the beans, prick the base with a fork, and brush with beaten egg. Return to the oven for a further 5 minutes.

Put the haddock and milk in a saucepan and bring to the boil, then reduce the heat and simmer for a further 10 minutes. Remove and skin the fish and flake into a bowl. Reserve the milk separately.

Heat the butter in a saucepan, add the onion and celery and cook gently until softened. Stir in the flour and cook for a couple of minutes, then add the reserved poaching milk and stir until the sauce has thickened. Season with a little salt, pepper and grated nutmeg. Remove from the heat and stir into the fish, adding the watercress and beaten eggs. Pour into the pastry case and sprinkle the top with the grated Parmesan. Bake in the oven for 25–30 minutes, when the tart will have risen and be crusted a delectable golden brown. Leave to cool slightly before turning out and eating hot.

Spinach and Anchovy Tart

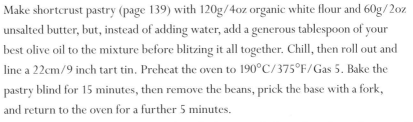

Perfect at any time of year, but plus-perfect in the spring, when you can buy or grow tiny pousse, the baby leaves of spinach that are gently, tenderly unferrous and don't exude copious amounts of liquid when you cook them. Spinach and anchovies: what can I say, other than that they are a heavenly marriage. Inspired by a soufflé, I set out to reproduce the taste in a tart. Curiously there is no battle, therefore no winner, no loser, between these two strong tastes when they're set in conjunction; the one doesn't cancel out the other, but enhances it. Just don't be tempted to add more anchovies than I've used in the recipe below, and don't add salt: the anchovies have it in spadefuls.

Serves 6
30g/1oz unsalted butter
1 tbsp olive oil
325g/12oz organic baby
    spinach
black pepper
200ml/7fl oz double cream
1 egg and 2 egg yolks
12 anchovy fillets

Make shortcrust pastry (page 139) with 120g/4oz organic white flour and 60g/2oz unsalted butter, but, instead of adding water, add a generous tablespoon of your best olive oil to the mixture before blitzing it all together. Chill, then roll out and line a 22cm/9 inch tart tin. Preheat the oven to 190°C/375°F/Gas 5. Bake the pastry blind for 15 minutes, then remove the beans, prick the base with a fork, and return to the oven for a further 5 minutes.

While the pastry is in the oven, heat the butter and olive oil in a heavy-bottomed enamel saucepan, add the spinach and pepper, and stir briefly until the spinach has wilted but not lost its shape, about a couple of minutes.

Whisk the cream, egg and yolks together, then pour in any liquid from the spinach pan. Tip the spinach and anchovies into a food processor and process as briefly as you dare, to keep their texture and not reduce them to a slushy purée. Throw them into the bowl with the cream and eggs and stir with a fork, then pour the whole lot into the pastry case and cook for about 25 minutes.

Leave to cool for 10 minutes, then serve with something plain, like a cherry tomato salad, and good, white country bread and butter, as I did for lunch this May Day Saturday.

ASPARAGUS TART

As soon as the first tender shoots of Evesham asparagus appear, I am done for. First I eat mounds of them, bare but for best unsalted butter dribbled extravagantly over them, and a grinding of coarse pepper. Then there comes a point where I can begin to bear sharing their flavour with others, not using them as the star turn. A dish of late spring vegetables perhaps, fresh peas, broad beans, asparagus and shallots brought together at the last moment, buttered and minted; a salad of asparagus, grilled red peppers, and the thinnest sliced raw fennel, red and green, cooked and raw combined in a lemony dressing; or an asparagus tart, all green spears and creaminess, tender, juicy, almost mellow.

Never, never think you can squeeze more out of each fragile wand than you really can. By that, I mean always chop every stem to where it starts feeling woody, and peel the lowest 3–4cm/inch or two just to be safe. I tend to chop the wands into generous 2–3cm/1 inch lengths, with the spears longer by their spear-head so to speak. Then, a golden rule which I try never to short-cut, steam the chopped stems for a few minutes before you throw the tender buds in after them; that way you won't get the flobby mess that putting them in together can lead to. The point of a sharp knife should pierce the flesh firmly but unresistantly. Then stop cooking immediately. One fat bundle of asparagus will fill your tart case. I think Parmesan is a great enhancer here, but you could be a purist and rest with cream and eggs.

Serves 6

22cm/9 inch shortcrust
  pastry case, chilled
  (page 139)
beaten egg, for brushing
1 good-sized bundle
  of asparagus
300ml/10fl oz cream
150ml/5fl oz Jersey milk
4 egg yolks
2 tbsp freshly grated
  Parmesan
salt and black pepper

Preheat the oven to 200°C/400°F/Gas 6. Bake the pastry blind for 15 minutes, then remove the beans, prick the base with a fork and return to the oven for 5 minutes. Remove the pastry case from the oven and brush with beaten egg. Turn the oven down to 180°C/350°F/Gas 4.

Steam the asparagus as discussed above and leave to cool. Whisk the cream, milk and egg yolks together, add the grated Parmesan and season. Spoon the cooled asparagus into the pastry case, then pour over the custard. Cook for 25–30 minutes, until puffed up and just set and browned.

Leave to cool for 10 minutes, then turn out and serve with a strong-noted salad, say raw fennel, orange and watercress with a walnut or hazelnut and olive oil dressing, which introduces astringence and pepperiness.

COURGETTE AND BASIL TART
WITH A RAW TOMATO DRESSING

The mild, fugitive flavour of the courgette flees altogether if it is introduced to water but, curiously, is brought out by the strongest of tastes. Think of ratatouille — where it finds its place perfectly — of basil, tomato, garlic, Parmesan, green olive oil, or tarragon, which would substitute beautifully for the basil here.

The courgettes have to be small, green-fingered and squeaky firm, the flowers just off them, for me to bother with. Once they're puffed up and waterily bloated, their insides like wet wood pulp, I don't want to know.

I don't put Parmesan or Gruyère in this tart, although they are perfect in a gratin of courgettes; I think they would overwhelm it. If you don't like the idea of a raw tomato dressing, you could make a simple mozzarella di bufala and tomato salad to serve at its side.

Serves 6
22cm/9 inch shortcrust
   pastry case, chilled
   (page 139)
800g/1¾lb small, firm
   courgettes
salt and black pepper
2–3 tbsp olive oil
2 eggs and 2 egg yolks
150–300ml/5–10fl oz
   double cream
a handful of basil leaves
   (about 4 tbsp)

Tomato dressing
1 small onion
1 clove of garlic
675g/1½lb tomatoes,
   skinned, seeded and
   finely chopped
6 tbsp olive oil
1 tbsp each of torn basil
   leaves, chopped chives
   and flat-leaf parsley
2 tbsp lemon juice
salt and black pepper

Preheat the oven to 190°C/375°F Gas 5. Bake the pastry blind for 15 minutes, then remove the beans, prick the base with a fork, and return to the oven for 5 minutes.

Slice the courgettes into thinnish coins and layer them in a colander, salting each layer. Leave to drain for 20–30 minutes, then rinse and dry on kitchen paper.

Heat the olive oil in a large, heavy-bottomed frying pan, throw in the courgettes, and cook until they are slightly softened and translucent, but do not allow them to colour. Remove from the pan and drain.

Whisk together the eggs, yolks, cream and seasoning: the amount of cream will depend on the depth of your tart tin, so begin with the smaller amount and add more if it doesn't look as if the mixture will fill the pastry case. Put the courgettes into the pastry case with the torn basil leaves, and pour over the egg and cream mixture. Bake until just set, puffed up and deliciously browned, about 30 minutes. Leave to cool for about 10 minutes before turning out, and eat while warm with the gutsy raw tomato dressing, made while the tart is in the oven.

Mince the onion and garlic together in a food processor. Put in a bowl with the remaining ingredients, stir, then cover and leave in the fridge for 20 minutes. Stir again, and spoon on to the plates alongside the tart.

TOMATO AND SAFFRON TART

When I first saw a recipe for a tomato and saffron quiche in Simon Hopkinson's lovely book *Gammon and Spinach*, *with the gently cajoling statement that it came a close second to his favourite quiche from Lorraine, it didn't take me long to get to work. The cut tart is as brazenly primary-coloured as you could hope for, with its sunset stripes of scarlet and yellow, and with one of the most soothing of saffrony custards imaginable. The texture is ambrosial.*

Like all tinkerers, I decided to change a few details, largely at the behest of my oldest daughter Miranda, whose critical faculties when it comes to judging tarts are nothing short of lethal. She demanded that I made it with the tomato sauce base that I use in my tomato and oatmeal tart, stating that the tinniness and texture of the tomatoes was not quite right. This is going to make more than double what you need, but I never see the point in making small quantities of fresh tomato sauce: it keeps well in the fridge for several days, or you can freeze it. Use it with cod, meatballs, pasta or what you will. Of course, adjust the quantity if you want to.

Serves 6
22cm/9 inch shortcrust
    pastry case, chilled
    (page 139)
beaten egg, for brushing
400ml/14fl oz double cream
1 tsp saffron threads,
    steeped in 1 tbsp hot water
    for at least 5 minutes
2 eggs and 4 egg yolks
1 dozen basil leaves
salt and black pepper

Fresh tomato sauce
3 tbsp olive oil
2 onions, 2 sticks of celery,
    6 cloves of garlic, finely
    chopped
1kg/2¼lb ripe tomatoes,
    skinned, seeded and
    chopped

Preheat the oven to 200°C/400°F/Gas 6. Bake the pastry blind for 15 minutes, then remove the beans, brush the pastry all over with beaten egg, and return to the oven for 10 minutes. Remove from the oven and leave to cool. Turn the heat down to 160°C/325°F/Gas 3 and put a large baking sheet into the oven.

For the tomato sauce, heat the oil in a large, heavy-bottomed frying pan and sauté the onions, celery and garlic until softened and translucent. Add the fresh and tinned tomatoes; chop the tinned ones once they're in the pan. Add the passata, tomato purée, bay leaves and sugar, then the red wine, and keep at a steady simmer for at least 30 minutes, until the sauce is thick and jammy and the liquid has evaporated. Remove the bay leaves.

You can either use it as it is, or, which I prefer, put it through the largest setting of a mouli-légumes to make a coarsely textured purée with enough bite to complement the heavenly, trembly custard that comes to rest on it. Leave to cool while you make the custard.

Put 4 tablespoons of the cream in a small saucepan with the saffron threads and their water. Heat until warm, then leave to infuse for 5 minutes. Beat together the eggs and yolks, and stir in the remaining cream and the saffron cream. Do this with

1 x 400g/14oz tin Italian
    plum tomatoes, organic
    if possible
200g/7oz organic tomato
    passata
1 tbsp tomato purée
2 bay leaves
2 tsp molasses sugar
150ml/5fl oz red wine
salt and black pepper

a fork: saffron threads wrap themselves around a whisk. Tear the basil into small pieces, stir into the custard, and season.

Spread a layer of the tomato mixture over the pastry, to come almost half-way up the pastry case. Put the tart with its tomato layer on to the heated baking sheet, on a rack slightly pulled out of the oven, then, using a jug, carefully pour in the saffron custard. Bake until the custard is tremblingly set — about 30 – 40 minutes — and an intense, goldy colour with brown patches. Allow to cool for at least 10 minutes before turning out and eating.

A thinly sliced raw fennel salad, coated in a dressing of best olive oil with a squeeze of lemon juice, is the only other thing you'll need.

TOMATO AND OATMEAL TART

There was a day, not so long ago, when vegetarianism meant nut cutlets, socks-and-sandals and sprouting mung beans. Lentil bake sat drying and crusting round the edges in wholefood restaurants, alongside earthy, solid, unrelieved plates of fibre, to which the words enjoyment, cuisine, were somehow strangers, unrelated. The food was too busy being good for you.

That even our best chefs and cooks now offer genuinely inventive vegetarian food, with no obvious sense of its being enforced tokenism, is as it should be. We flesh-eaters can all be vegetarians on our nights off, and the socks and sandals brigade can smarten up their act and serve us something we might actually want to eat.

This tart is enough to convert even the most recidivist of meat and two veggers. It is one of the greats. I have served it at a 'big girls' lunch' and had everyone begging for the recipe, and it is a wonderful picnic tart, the sturdier pastry a better container than thin shortcrust.

Serves 8–10
1 organic egg
150ml/5fl oz double cream
1 tbsp each of grated
   Parmesan and Gruyère
2 tbsp grated mature Cheddar
salt and black pepper
fresh thyme

Tomato sauce
See page 48. You might
like to add 1 tbsp each of
fresh thyme, flat-leaf parsley
and basil

Make shortcrust pastry in the normal way (page 139), but use 120g/4oz organic white flour, 120g/4oz organic porridge oats and 120g/4oz unsalted butter. Chill, then roll out just a little thicker than for normal shortcrust and line a 30cm/ 12 inch greased tart tin. Reserve the remaining pastry in strips for a lattice or, if you can't be bothered, save it for another tart. Preheat the oven to 190°C/ 375°F/Gas 5. Bake the pastry blind for 10 minutes, then remove the beans, prick the base with a fork, and return to the oven for 5 minutes.

Make the tomato sauce as on page 48; if you like, you could reverse the proportions of fresh and canned tomatoes. Add the thyme and parsley with the bay leaves and simmer, uncovered, until the sauce is beginning to thicken, stirring occasionally for about 15 minutes. Add a good splash of wine, season, and simmer for another 30 minutes or so, giving it the odd stir, and adding a bit more wine if it dries out. Sprinkle with the torn basil when it has cooled down a bit.

Whisk the egg and cream together, then whisk in the Parmesan, Gruyère and half the Cheddar. Season and scatter in a few thyme leaves. Spread a thick layer of tomato sauce over the pastry to come half-way up the pastry case, then pour over the custard. Arrange your pastry lattice over the top and sprinkle with the remaining Cheddar. Bake for about 25 minutes, until set and palely browned. Leave to cool for about 10 minutes before serving.

HERB TART

This tart is either brilliant by design — in late spring when all the herbs are rushing with growth and intensely flavoured — or when the cupboard is bare, and all you can find are the basics: eggs, cream, milk and flour and whatever you've got growing in your herb garden. Any combination of the ones listed below makes a good tart, and a thrifty dinner.

Serves 6
22cm/9 inch shortcrust
    pastry case, chilled
    (page 139)
beaten egg, for brushing
30g/1oz unsalted butter
1 heaped tbsp each of
    chopped flat-leaf parsley,
    tarragon, basil, thyme,
    chives and chervil
2 eggs and 2 egg yolks
450ml/15fl oz double
    cream, or half cream and
    half Jersey milk
salt, black pepper, nutmeg
120g/4oz Gruyère or
    Emmental, grated
2 tbsp coarsely grated
    Parmesan (optional)

Preheat the oven to 190°C/375°F/Gas 5. Bake the pastry blind for 15 minutes, then remove the beans, prick the base with a fork, and return to the oven for 5 minutes. Brush with beaten egg and leave to cool.

Heat the butter in a frying pan, add the herbs and stir briefly to coat. In a large bowl, whisk together the eggs, yolks and cream or cream and milk, season with salt, pepper and a suspicion of grated nutmeg, then stir in the Gruyère or Emmental. Stir in the herbs, then pour the mixture into the pastry case and cook for about 25–30 minutes. After about 15 minutes you can sprinkle over a couple of tablespoons of coarsely grated Parmesan if you like a cheesier flavour. Leave to cool for about 10 minutes before serving.

Brown Onion and Basil Pissaladière

This makes a wonderful summer lunch: a tangle of onions browned in balsamic vinegar and spicy green globe basil, with giant Napoletana basil torn over the tomato topping. Of course use ordinary basil if that's all you can find. You can buy small amounts of fresh yeast from most good bakers — or ask for it at the bakery counter of your supermarket.

Serves 5 – 6

Dough

30g/1oz fresh yeast

salt

300g/10oz pasta flour
  (I used Doves Farm Type
  '0' pasta flour)

90g/3oz butter

2 eggs

Topping

olive oil

just under 1kg/2lb organic
  onions, thinly sliced

2 tbsp best balsamic vinegar

2 heaped tsp molasses
  sugar

a good handful of basil
  (see introduction)

salt and black pepper

2 x 50g/1¾oz tins of
  anchovies, drained

4 cloves of new garlic

6 organic tomatoes, skinned
  and sliced

I made my dough in a food processor with the dough hook, but it is easy by hand. Dissolve the yeast in 4 – 5 tablespoons of tepid water with a pinch of salt. Sift the flour, add the butter in small pieces, and process briefly, or rub in using your fingertips. Make a well in the centre and add the eggs and the yeast mixture. Process until the dough comes away from the bowl in a ball. (If making the dough by hand, mix the eggs and yeast with the flour, gradually drawing the flour in from around the edge of the well, then knead lightly until the dough comes together.) Put it on a floured plate, cover with a floured cloth and leave somewhere warm for 2 hours.

For the topping, heat a few tablespoons of olive oil in a large, heavy-bottomed frying pan, add the onions and cook gently until translucent. Add the balsamic vinegar, molasses sugar and basil leaves – ideally green globe basil – keeping a few leaves back to scatter over the pissaladière when it comes out of the oven. Season, and stir until glossily browned all over, then cover the pan and leave it, but for the occasional stir, for 30 minutes. Pound the anchovies with the peeled garlic.

Preheat the oven to 190°C/375°F/Gas 5. After 2 hours the dough will have doubled in size. Knock it back, knead it briefly, then put it in the middle of an olive-oiled baking sheet, about 35 x 22cm/14 x 9 inches. Press the dough out with your knuckles to cover the sheet, spread the onion mixture evenly over the surface, then the anchovy mixture, and leave the dough to rise for a further 15 minutes.

Cook in the centre of the oven for 20 minutes, then turn the heat down to 180°C/350°F/Gas 4 and cook for a further 15 – 20 minutes. Remove from the oven and lay the slices of tomato over the onions. Tear the reserved basil leaves into pieces – this is where I have used giant Napoletana basil when I have been able to get hold of it – and scatter over the top. Dribble over a little olive oil, slice, and eat hot-and-cold in your fingers.

Sweetcorn and Spring Onion Tart with a Polenta Crust

You can of course make this tart with ordinary shortcrust but, much as I hate faffed-about-with food, this crust is a stunning yellow colour, with corn's characteristic slight grittiness, and with the fresh corn kernels it is doubly corny! The milky sweetness of fresh, plump buds of corn is not quite enough on its own, so I gently sautéed some spring onions in butter, and the tart's essential mildness had a counterpoint. This really is a good dish on a day when you want something wholesome that isn't aggressive tasting. Early autumn is obviously the natural time for it, when the first small cobs of corn are at their tenderly sweetest, sheltering kernels that are spurting with milk.

Serves 6

150g/5oz organic quick-
  cooking polenta (Biona
  make a good one)
a pinch of sea salt
2 bunches of spring onions
  (outer skins removed),
  finely chopped
a knob of butter
2 eggs and 2 egg yolks
300ml/10fl oz double cream
2 corn cobs, cooked, with
  the kernels stripped off
  on to a plate
salt, black pepper, cayenne

Preheat the oven to 180°C/350°F/Gas 4.

For the polenta crust, simply bring 300ml/½ pint of water to the boil in a saucepan and slowly pour in the polenta. Throw a pinch of sea salt after it, and stir over a gentle heat for 5 minutes. Remove from the heat and form the polenta into a ball. Using a bit of flour – not polenta, which would make the finished crust too gritty – roll out in the normal way to line a 22cm/9 inch tart tin, remembering that, unlike flour-based pastry, this is good-tempered enough to be pressed into the tin if it breaks anywhere. Prick the base and bake for 10 minutes. You don't need to bake it blind with beans.

Sauté the spring onions in the butter until softened and translucent. Whisk together the eggs, yolks and cream, then add the spring onions together with the corn kernels. Season carefully – there should be enough cayenne to give it warmth, but not overpower – and pour the mixture into the pastry case. Bake for 25–30 minutes until golden, puffed up and just set. Leave to cool for 10 minutes before serving, accompanied by peppery watercress or landcress with a garlicky dressing.

HOMITY PIES

I remember eating Homity Pies years ago in the original Cranks restaurant in Marshall Street, just behind Carnaby Street. I first attempted my own version of them — without the mushrooms which I remember in the original — when my two oldest children were tiny. I really favour a wholemeal crust here, but it is entirely up to you. They are brilliant picnic food: substantial and not prone to disintegrate in the lap. We take them, well wrapped in foil, on the way to Ireland, and they still have that lovely memory of warmth about them even after hours in the car.

Serves 6

shortcrust pastry made with 180g/6oz flour and 90g/3oz butter (page 139), chilled

325g/12oz potatoes

30g/1oz butter

3–4 tbsp milk or cream

450g/1lb onions, finely chopped

3 tbsp olive oil

2 cloves of garlic, crushed

2 tbsp chopped flat-leaf parsley, or mixed parsley, chives and thyme

120g/4oz mature Cheddar, grated

salt and black pepper

2 ripe tomatoes, thinly sliced

Roll out the pastry thinly and use it to line six individual greased tart tins, 10cm/ 4 inches in diameter. If you don't have individual tins, make one large tart in a 30cm/12 inch tin. Preheat the oven to 220°C/425°F/Gas 7. Bake the pastry blind for 10 minutes in the smaller tins, 15 in the large one. Remove the beans and return the pastry to the oven for 5 minutes.

Boil the potatoes until cooked, drain, then mash them with the butter and milk or cream. Sauté the onions in the olive oil until golden and softened. Stir into the potato mixture with the garlic, herbs, half the cheese and the seasoning. Leave to cool until at least tepid.

Fill the pastry cases with the mixture, sprinkle with the remaining cheese and place a slice of tomato on top of each tart. Bake for 20 minutes, until gratinéed and goldenly bubbling. Leave to cool slightly before eating or wrapping in foil for a picnic.

BREAKFAST TART

This started off as a joke, but then it got serious. Having declared authoritatively that there wasn't an occasion or time of day at which a tart wouldn't please and delight, I got to thinking about breakfast. Serious breakfast. The full monty sort of breakfast: eggs, bacon, black pudding, grilled tomatoes. The accompanying toast is, like pasta, the vehicle on which the rich, succulently flavoured proteins travel best, so why not encase the whole thing in pastry instead? The result was glorious, a great brunch, or lunch or supper if you think it's a p.m. sort of a tart.

The secret is not to turn it into a mobile junkyard, and not to overstuff it, or the individual flavours lose out. Mushrooms, I feel, are a flavour too far, but you might prefer them if you are not a black pudding convert like me. My inspiration was dotting the tart with cherry tomatoes rolled in olive oil and warmed in the oven first. They burst on to the tongue with flavour, and cut a dash through all the rich, eggy, meaty protein.

Serves 6
22cm/9 inch shortcrust
  pastry case, chilled
  (page 139)
beaten egg, for brushing
2–3 rashers of oak-smoked
  organic bacon
3 slices of black pudding
a nut of butter
12–15 organic cherry
  tomatoes
about ½ tbsp olive oil
1 egg and 2 egg yolks
  (I used duck eggs)
200ml/7fl oz organic double
  cream
3 tbsp Jersey milk (optional)
black pepper

Preheat the oven to 200°C/400°F/Gas 6. Bake the pastry blind for 10 minutes, then remove the beans, prick the base with a fork, brush with beaten egg and return to the oven for 5 minutes. Remove from the oven and turn the heat down to 180°C/350°F/Gas 4. Meanwhile, prepare the filling.

Snip the bacon into pieces and cook without additional fat in a small frying pan until crisply frizzled. Drain on kitchen paper. Fry the black pudding in the butter until browned on both sides. Drain. Cut the black pudding slices into quarters. Put the tomatoes in a heatproof bowl and pour the olive oil over them. Shake to coat, and put them in the oven for 10 minutes.

Whisk the eggs and cream – and milk if you're using it – together and season with pepper. I thinned my custard down with milk since I was using richer eggs; the duck eggs turned the tart a heavenly golden colour.

Scatter the black pudding and bacon over the pastry, then add the tomatoes strategically, and gently place the tart on a baking sheet on the oven rack. Pour in the custard carefully from a jug, and slide the baking sheet into the oven. Cook for about 35 minutes. Leave to cool for 10 minutes before turning out and serving.

I can't think of a suitable accompaniment other than ketchup or brown sauce if you feel the urge, and a cup of tea!

"It is difficult to meet an ungenerous cook. The very heart of the experience of making food is about sharing, nurture, generosity, the giving of pleasure."

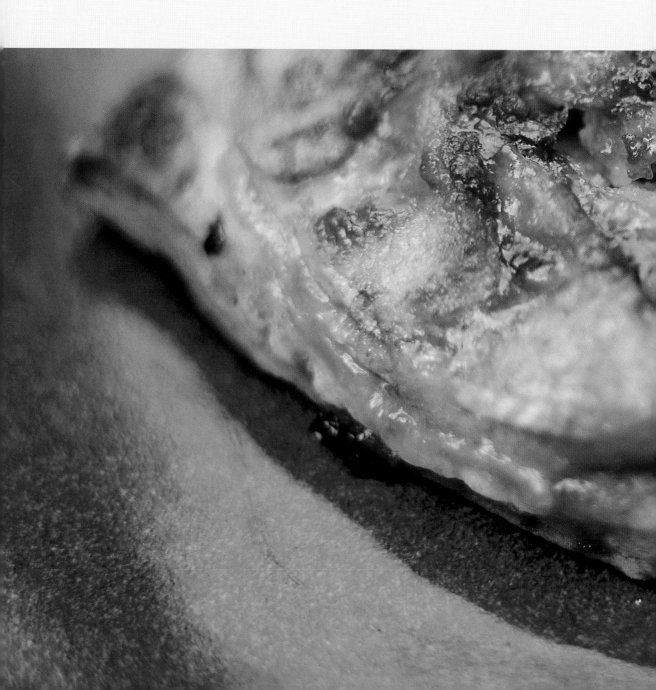

OTHER PEOPLE'S TARTS

Richard Corrigan's Banana Tart (page 78)

Broccoli, Blue Cheese and Crème Fraîche Tart

No one has done as much as Nigel Slater in the way of making people just want to cook, and in inspiring the confidence to do so. His columns are rich, delicious and, like all the best food, wickedly sexy. His food writing is totally seductive.

I went to interview him for Food Illustrated, *and spent a blissful few hours talking to him about his childhood, his career, and the writing that evokes in his readers the pleasure and comfort of knowing that he's really just one of them, simply hungering after a good dinner. 'I want people to relax and stop thinking they've got to put on a show. The nicest things are the simplest.' I think his heart really is in baking, which he began to learn about after his mother's death when he was a boy of nine. The afternoon I spent with him, he'd made scones, and the most delicious, crumbly, buttery, lavender biscuits, with the sort of taste you want to bottle. Try this tart of his; it is perfect as a light lunch or supper.*

Serves 6 – 8

150g/5oz broccoli, ideally
    purple sprouting
3 tbsp olive oil
1 medium onion, finely sliced
a few sprigs of thyme
4 cloves of garlic, peeled
4 anchovy fillets, chopped
90g/3oz pungent blue
    cheese such as
    Gorgonzola or Fourme
    d'Ambert
1 tsp capers, rinsed
200ml/7floz crème fraîche
black pepper
350g/13oz puff pastry
    (chilled ready-rolled
    is fine here)
Parmesan for grating

Preheat the oven to 220°C/425°F/Gas 7.

Rinse the broccoli thoroughly and drop it into boiling, salted water. Leave it to cook until tender – about 7 minutes depending on the type. Drain, pat dry on kitchen paper and set aside. Return the empty saucepan to the heat and add the olive oil, onion, thyme and the garlic cloves. Leave them to stew to softness over a moderate heat. They should be golden and tender after 10 minutes or so.

Chop the drained broccoli roughly and add it to the onions with the chopped anchovies, crumbled cheese, capers and crème fraîche. Grind in a little pepper and then leave the mixture to cool.

Open up the pastry, or roll your own into a 35 x 22cm/14 x 9 inch rectangle, and place it on a lightly floured baking sheet. Score a line, without going right through the pastry, along all four sides, about 3cm/1 inch from the edge. Spread the broccoli mixture over the centre of the pastry, taking it as far as the lines you have scored, and leaving a clear border. This will rise and form a rim during cooking. Scatter with grated Parmesan.

Bake for 15 – 20 minutes. Check after 15; it will cook very quickly. You want the edges to be dark golden brown and crisp. Serve at once, with a salad on the side.

George Morley's Leek Tart

I first met George (Georgina) when my agent George (Georgina) was perambulating me around the publishers trying to sell my book Last Letters Home. *I remember saying to agent George, 'She is the only one I really want to work with.' It was obvious that George really wanted to do the book – she doesn't hide her enthusiasm under a bushel – and there is nothing more confidence-inspiring to the doubtful writer than the enthusiasm and belief of a good editor. Luckily, George's bosses at Macmillan agreed, and thence began an extremely happy partnership, which nowadays is confined to greedy weekends rather than work.*

There is no one I am happier working with in a kitchen. George is obsessively knowledge-able, and equally as greedy as me, and when she comes to stay with her husband Shawn and young son Charlie, we plan the food in slavering telephone calls. I'd like to think we inspire each other to greater heights of culinary achievement. Not that we aim for kitchen pyrotechnics, but we do like to bask in cooking the unknown, untested delight for each other, a discreet bit of one-upmanship, or, if people are coming, perform an extraordinarily harmonious double act in the small space that is my kitchen. I know that if she says 'What about a caramelized apple pavlova?' she will get stuck in and do it, and it will be sublime.

Serves 6–8
1.35kg/3lb leeks
large knob of butter
  (about 120g/4 oz!)
200ml/7fl oz sour cream
2 eggs, beaten
salt, black pepper, paprika

Cheese pastry
90g/3oz strong Cheddar,
  grated
90g/3oz butter
240g/8oz plain flour
a pinch of salt
beaten egg, for brushing

For the cheese pastry (which is basically Arabella Boxer's recipe), process the cheese and butter into the flour with the salt. Add iced water slowly until the mixture comes together. Leave to rest in the fridge for at least an hour, then roll out and line a 25cm/10 inch tart tin. Preheat the oven to 200°C/400°F/Gas 6. Brush the pastry with a little beaten egg and bake blind (no need for baking beans) for 15–20 minutes. Turn the heat down to 180°C/350°F/Gas 4.

Slice the leeks and rinse if gritty. Discard any really tough dark green bits. Sweat the leeks in a very generous knob of butter until completely softened, but do not let them brown. Leave to cool slightly.

Mix the sour cream with the beaten eggs and add the leeks. Season with salt and pepper and shake in enough paprika to turn the mixture a very pale rusty pink – about ½ a teaspoon should do it. Pour into the pastry case and bake for about 20 minutes, or until just set. It should be wobbly in the middle. Best served about 15 minutes after it emerges from the oven, when it is still warm but not piping hot.

COUSIN DEBORAH'S CHEESE STRATA

Deborah and I are first cousins and have enjoyed food together since our childhood Sunday lunches with our mutual grandparents in Sussex. Their cook, Rhoda, would usually have a gargantuan sirloin or baron of beef brought to the table, often with a turkey in case that's what the grandchildren preferred, and at least six vegetables from the amazing kitchen garden. And then there were the puddings: cloud-topped lemon meringue pies, treacle tarts, steamed chocolate puddings, lemon mousses, with jugs of thick ivory cream. We still talk about those lunches, and have kept on the tradition for our children, who all appreciate good food and, thank God, like each other independently of the fact that they happen to be cousins. Deborah is an exceptionally fine cook, wonderful to work with in the kitchen, and I don't believe we've ever quarrelled in or out of it. When she brought her boys Alexander and Oliver out to Ireland last summer we cooked frenziedly for five days, relishing the chatter, the greed and the absence of pressure when two equals equal half the work.

There is no pastry here, but in every other aspect it meets my demands of a fine savoury tart: cheesy, eggy, creamy, self-contained and great to serve after the theatre or a movie, with a salad. It is refrigerated for 24 hours before cooking, so plan ahead.

Serves 6 but can be stretched
120g/4oz thinly sliced
    streaky bacon
1 tsp olive oil
1 medium onion, chopped
    very small
about 90g/3oz butter,
    softened
5 slices of good-quality one-
    day-old bread
180g/6oz mature Cheddar,
    grated
4 eggs, beaten lightly
450ml/15fl oz single cream
¼ tsp paprika
¼ tsp chilli powder
1 tsp mustard powder

Fry the bacon in the olive oil until crisp, drain it on kitchen paper and chop it into small pieces. Fry the onion in the same pan until soft, but not coloured, then remove with a slotted spoon.

Butter the bread on one side, and cut into cubes. Line a 23cm/11 inch flan dish with half the bread cubes. Sprinkle with half the cheese. Put the rest of the bread into the flan dish and scatter over the rest of the cheese. Whisk together the eggs, cream and spices, and pour them over the top. Refrigerate for 24 hours.

Preheat the oven to 180°C/350°F/Gas 4. Bake the strata for an hour and leave to stand for 5–10 minutes before serving.

This is also delicious with lightly poached haddock between the layers of bread, and sautéed mushrooms rather than bacon.

SLOW-ROASTED TOMATO TART

I bumped into Celia Brooks Brown in my favourite cookery book shop. Books for Cooks, in Blenheim Crescent in Notting Hill, makes the amateur, the ingenue, the serious and the professional cook feel at home. There is always someone knowledgeable to give advice, help with a query, trace a difficult-to-find tome, or put one on to something utterly new and inspiring. I spend whole mornings there, infrequently, but they are invaluable for research, inspiration, ideas, and for making one realize how frighteningly much more there is to learn. There is a little café at the back, where cooks come in on a rota basis and make lunch. If you can get a table, you are likely to be fed by a fledgling or fully fledged cook, say, trying out recipes for a new book. This morning, Celia was making a Black Forest meringue, with cherries on stalks sunken glossily into the cream. We got talking, and I ended up buying her book Vegetarian Foodscape, *from which this recipe comes.*

Serves 6
22cm/9 inch shortcrust
   pastry case, chilled
   (page 139)
beaten egg white, for brushing
1.35kg/3lb ripe plum
   tomatoes
6 cloves of garlic,
   sliced wafer thin
4 tbsp olive oil
2 tbsp balsamic vinegar
salt and black pepper
a little sugar
3 egg yolks
150ml/5fl oz crème fraîche
2 handfuls of basil leaves

Preheat the oven to 190°C/375°F/Gas 5. Bake the pastry blind for 15 minutes, then remove the beans and return to the oven for 5 minutes. Brush egg white over the pastry and leave to cool. Turn the heat down to 150°C/300°F/Gas 2.

Place the tomatoes in a bowl and pour boiling water over them. Spike each one with the point of a knife, and drain after 1 minute. Pour cold water over them and drain it off immediately; they will now be cool enough to handle. Slip them out of their skins, slice them in half vertically, and place them cut side up in a roasting dish. Lay the garlic slices inside the tomato halves. Dribble the olive oil and balsamic vinegar into the halves and sprinkle with salt, pepper and a little sugar. Roast in the oven for about 1 hour, until shrunken and brown around the edges.

Arrange the roasted tomatoes in the pastry case, adding any juices from the roasting dish. Mix together the egg yolks and crème fraîche, and tear in the basil leaves. Season with salt and pepper and pour the mixture over the tomatoes. Bake for 30–40 minutes, until the custard is set and lightly browned. Leave to stand for 10 minutes before turning out and serving.

TOMATO TARTE TATIN

Lindsey Bareham's The Big Red Book of Tomatoes *is a compendium of wonderful tomato recipes gathered from around the world — or all the countries where the tomato is as staple an ingredient as the potato, which she has also written a definitive book about. What I like about her unpretentious writing is how she elevates humble ingredients thriftily, imaginatively, into the most delicious recipes. She would always use the best olive oil, the best ham, but every extravagance is carefully considered within the context of creating wonderful food reasonably. We met when I went to interview her about the book, having not seen each other for 25 years, since I briefly went out with her brother.*

Serves 4

1 heaped tsp caster sugar
salt and black pepper
1 tbsp balsamic vinegar
4 tbsp olive oil
800g/1¾lb medium
  tomatoes, skinned,
  cored, and halved through
  the cores
150g/5oz puff pastry

To serve

30g/1oz Parmesan
a few basil leaves

Preheat the oven to 200°C/400°F/Gas 6. Lightly oil an 18cm/7 inch tart tin.

Dissolve the sugar and a little salt and pepper in the vinegar, then whisk in 3 tablespoons of the olive oil. Place the tomato halves, rounded sides down, in the tin, nudging them close together so that they are slightly on their sides. Pour the dressing over the top.

On a floured surface, roll the pastry quite thinly and lay over the top of the tin. Cut round the edge, and lightly tuck the pastry down the sides like a blanket. Brush the remaining olive oil over the top of the pastry. Bake for about 20 minutes, until the pastry is puffed and scorched.

Remove from the oven and run a knife round the edge of the pastry. Carefully drain most of the liquid into a small bowl. Place a large plate over the tart tin and quickly invert. Set aside to cool slightly.

To serve, whisk the dressing and spoon it over the tomatoes. Grate over the Parmesan, snip over the basil, and slice the tart into four wedges. This is very good eaten with peas mixed with pesto that has been slackened with a little olive oil.

CHERRY TOMATO TARTE TATIN

Serves 4
200g/7oz puff pastry
4 tbsp extra virgin olive oil
about 500g/1¼lb organic
  cherry tomatoes,
  stalks removed
8 tbsp balsamic vinegar
port or Madeira (optional)
salt and black pepper

Preheat the oven to 220°C/425°F/Gas 7. Divide the puff pastry into four and roll into very thin 12cm/5 inch discs, or one large disc. Pour 1 tablespoon of the oil into each of four 10cm/4 inch tart tins, or into a 20cm/8 inch tart tin, swirl it around, then arrange the tomatoes in a single layer.

Heat the balsamic vinegar in a small saucepan and reduce until sticky and caramelized, adding a splash of port or Madeira if you have it to hand. Season the tomatoes with salt and pepper, then pour over a dribble of the vinegar. Cover with a pastry disc, tucking the pastry in at the sides. Bake for 8–10 minutes, until the pastry is puffed and golden. Check assiduously; a larger tart will take longer.

Remove from the oven and run a knife around the edge of the pastry. Place a plate over each tart tin and quickly invert. *Faites attention*! There could be quite a lot of liquid surrounding the tarts, like so many brown moats.

Blue Cheese Tarts
with Red Onion Marmalade

I can't remember when I first went to Markwick's, Judy and Stephen Markwick's wonderful restaurant in Bristol, but I have never had a bad meal there, and if you think that sounds like faint praise, I have only ever eaten exceptionally well there over the years. Stephen's set lunch used to be the best value I know; now that I no longer work in Bristol I only ever go to dinner there. He is, quite simply, a very good cook. Stephen is in the kitchen, not dancing table attendance or on television. Judy is out there talking to the customers, and gently but knowledgeably steering them through the wine list and the menu.

Serves 6

60g/2oz mascarpone

60ml/2fl oz double cream

3 egg yolks

180g/6oz blue cheese,
    crumbled (a mixture of
    Roquefort, Stilton and
    Shropshire Blue)

salt, black pepper and
    a pinch of cayenne

Red onion marmalade

2 red onions, thinly sliced

a pinch of salt, black pepper
    and sugar

60g/2oz butter

2 tbsp sherry vinegar

4 tbsp red wine

Preheat the oven to 190°C/375°F/Gas 5. Line six individual tart tins with either puff pastry (see page 141) or shortcrust pastry made with 120g/4oz flour (page 139), and bake blind. Remove from the oven and turn the heat up to 220°C/425°F/Gas 7.

Make the red onion marmalade by mixing the onions in a bowl with salt, pepper and sugar. Heat the butter in a saucepan until foamy and add the onions, stirring well. When almost cooked down, add the vinegar and red wine, and simmer gently until well reduced; this will take about 40–50 minutes.

Make the tart filling by beating together the mascarpone, cream and egg yolks until smooth, then stir in the blue cheese and seasoning. Place a spoonful of the onion marmalade into each pastry case (you can also add wilted spinach leaves if you like) and then fill each one with the blue cheese mixture. Bake for about 10–15 minutes. Good served with chutney, something like green tomato.

Sutlu Börek
Creamy Cheese Bake with Filo Pastry

This is not strictly a tart, but recently I went to the launch of Claudia Roden's book Tamarind and Spice, *where she cooked so many wonderful dishes I decided I couldn't leave her out of this book. I think her influence has been profound, starting with her original* Book of Middle Eastern Food *back in 1968. Nobody, she told me, wrote down recipes in Egypt when she was a girl there, everything was passed down from grandmother and mother to daughter. Claudia didn't even realize that her family ate Jewish Egyptian food until she left to come to London as an art student. She is both food writer and cultural historian, whose record of the traditional food and cooking of the Jewish people is a work of extraordinary scholarship and dedication, both fascinating and accessible, as is all her food writing. This is a Turkish recipe, with leaves of filo pastry baked with a light, creamy custard.*

Serves 4

150g/5oz feta cheese
150g/5oz cottage cheese
4 large eggs
3 tbsp chopped flat-leaf
  parsley
200g/7oz/5 large sheets
  filo pastry
30g/1oz unsalted butter,
  melted
450ml/15fl oz milk

Preheat the oven to 180°C/350°F/Gas 4.

To prepare the filling, mash the feta with a fork and mix with the cottage cheese, one egg and the parsley.

Open out the sheets of filo, leaving them in a pile. Brush the top one lightly with melted butter and then fit it, buttered side up, into an oiled round baking dish about 30cm/12 inches in diameter, leaving it overhanging at the sides. Fit the second sheet over it and brush lightly with butter. Spread the filling evenly over the pastry. Cover with the remaining sheets of filo, brushing each with melted butter and finally folding them over the mixture. Fold the top one so that it presents a smooth surface and brush with butter. Bake for 15 minutes until lightly coloured, then remove from the oven.

Lightly beat the remaining three eggs with the milk and pour over the hot pie; you do not need to add salt as the feta is very salty. Return to the oven and bake for about 30 minutes or until the custard is absorbed and set and the top of the pastry is golden. Serve hot, cut into wedges.

FEUILLÉTÉ AUX POIRES

This is the tart, if such a word is up to describing this stratospherically brilliant creation, that changed my teenage perception of food overnight. It is, retrospectively, something that has had an extraordinary influence on my cooking life, showing me, as it did, a level of cooking that went beyond anything I had suspected possible, yet remaining trenchantly rooted in the real world of achievable, good honest cooking.

When I first wrote to Pierre Koffmann's office to ask if I could have the recipe, I was informed that I certainly could, but as he was in transit between restaurants and homes, I would have to wait. Several months and several calls later, I decided on a more direct approach, and rang my culinary hero at The Berkeley. He rang me back, and charmingly explained what to do, all of 25 years after I had first tasted it! I think reinterpreting Monsieur Koffmann's description would be sacrilegious, so am breaking with tradition and reproducing the conversation we had as faithfully as possible. How you poach your pear and make your caramel I leave to you. My pear goes into a vanilla-sugared syrupy bath with a touch of lemon, and is poached until cooked.

'Cut the puff pastry out around the shape of the pear, and cook it until it is just done. Then, with the tip of a knife, cut round the bottom of the pastry, and remove the inside, leaving the bottom layer. Return to the oven for 3–5 minutes to dry out. Fill the pastry case with crème légère when it is cool – crème pâtissière with the same amount of whipped cream added to it – then put your poached pear half on top.'

'I seem to remember a sabayon with some eau de vie de poires?'

'Well, you wouldn't put that over the top because of the texture of the caramel [a thin layer of which he covers the pear with], but you might put it underneath, or you could add a drop of Poires Williams to the crème légère instead. If you have any problem, please ring again.'

And with that he was gone.

Thank you Monsieur Koffmann. In your quiet, unshowy way you have set the standard in London for two decades, and never resorted to the brash celebrity chef publicity stunts that so many have. We know that you are still in your kitchen, and that your food is as suffused with brilliance as it is with honesty.

MEYER LEMON TARTS

I met the inimitable Jeffrey Steingarten in New York last October, and attempted to interview him for Food Illustrated. *Jeffrey doesn't answer questions, like all good lawyers, he just tells you what he wants to tell you. Before he became US* Vogue's *food critic, and wrote the wonderful* The Man Who Ate Everything, *he was indeed a Harvard lawyer. Small detail is, alongside food, the staff of Jeffrey's life, and he told me the following: 'Frank Meyer introduced the eponymous lemon to America in 1905. He was an agricultural adventurist who'd found one growing in a pot in Peking. They are like Sicilian lemons, sweeter, less acid and more full of flavour than most lemons. They don't grow on the east coast of America, but I grow them in San Diego.' You will have to use a good organic lemon: southern Spanish are particularly good.*

Makes 6 individual tarts
190g/6½oz cold unsalted
    butter
1 large egg yolk
50g/1¾oz icing sugar
1 tbsp and a bit of
    double cream
240g/8oz unbleached flour

Meyer lemon cream filling
4 Meyer lemons
225g/7½oz vanilla caster
    sugar
4 large eggs
175ml/6fl oz cold double
    cream

Make the pastry in a food processor: blend the butter, egg yolk, icing sugar and cream until smooth (about 30 seconds), scraping down half-way through and at the end. Add the flour and blend just until the dough becomes a ball, about 5 seconds more. Break into six pieces, flatten them, wrap and refrigerate for about an hour.

On a floured surface, roll each piece out to a rough circle about 15cm/6 inches across and 3 mm/⅛ inch thick. Prick holes with a fork all over the dough. With a palette knife or spatula, lift a circle of dough and drape it over an individual flan ring, 10cm/4 inches in diameter and 2cm/⅞ inch high. Gently coax the dough down into the ring without stretching it. Now, rotating the ring as you go, push straight down along its sides so that the dough closely lines the bottom and sides. Do the same with five more rings. Set them on a baking sheet lined with parchment paper. Freeze for at least 30 minutes before baking.

Preheat the oven to 190°C/375°F/Gas 5. Bake the pastry for 15–18 minutes, until golden. With a spatula, transfer the pastry shells to a wire rack, and remove the rings with tongs.

For the filling, lightly grate the yellow skin of three of the lemons. Squeeze the juice of all four. Put the sugar and lemon zest in a saucepan. Whisk in the eggs and lemon juice. Heat gently, stirring constantly with a whisk, until the mixture thickens and pales. Immediately strain the mixture through a sieve into a bowl. Let it cool to room temperature, stirring occasionally. Whisk the cream until stiff, and fold it into the cooled custard. Spoon the mixture into the pastry shells.

CHERRY AND ALMOND TART

I was alerted to this tart through Simon Hopkinson's column in the Independent, *on a week when he was writing about 'absolute and cherished favourites.' That was enough for me. Simon is one of the select band of food writers who has had a huge influence on my food over the years, and who actually writes in a way that impels one to cook the recipe just as soon as one can lay one's hands on the ingredients. He is the kind of person who I know I would enjoy sitting down to a good dinner with; his passion for food is infectious.*

This tart is one he poached from Malcolm Reid and Colin Long, erstwhile proprietors of the famous Box Tree at Ilkley in Yorkshire, which I, like Simon, unfortunately never ate at. He describes this recipe of theirs as 'one of their most simple and impeccable.' He is right.

Serves 6 – 8
120g/4oz plain flour
60g/2oz butter, cut
   into cubes
a pinch of salt
1 egg yolk
1 – 2 tbsp iced water
a little beaten egg
2 rounded tbsp apricot jam

Filling
120g/4oz unsalted butter,
   softened
120g/4oz caster sugar,
   plus extra for serving
2 large eggs
120g/4oz ground almonds
grated zest of 1 lemon
400g/14oz (drained weight)
   stoned, bottled morello
   cherries

In a food processor, blend together the flour, butter and salt, then tip them into a large bowl and gently mix in the egg yolk and water with cool hands or a knife, until well amalgamated. Chill in the fridge for at least an hour.

Preheat the oven to 190°C/375°F/Gas 5. Line a 22cm/9 inch tart tin with the pastry and bake blind for 15 – 20 minutes. Remove the beans, brush the pastry with beaten egg and return to the oven for a further 10 minutes, until it is golden, crisp and well cooked, particularly the base. Warm the jam slightly and spoon over the base of the tart. Leave to cool. Turn the heat down to 180°C/350°F/Gas 4.

For the filling, beat together the butter and sugar until light and fluffy. Add one egg and continue beating until it is entirely incorporated, then add the other egg and beat again. Add the ground almonds and lemon zest and fold them in thoroughly. Spoon into the pastry case and smooth the top. Press the cherries into the mixture, pushing them under the almond paste with your fingers.

Return to the oven and bake for 40 minutes or so, until the surface is golden brown, puffed up and springy to the touch. Switch off the oven and leave the tart there with the door ajar for 15 minutes. Dust with caster sugar before serving.

APRICOT FRANGIPANE TART

In an ideal world, I'd live so close to Baker & Spice in Walton Street (see page 141) that I could smell the yeasty baking smells all day. They are quite simply the best baker and pâtissier I know this side of the Channel. No croissants get near theirs: flaky, buttery, with an almost sandy, grainy texture, light yet substantial, with that wonderful stretchy, lycra-ey core that resists being pulled apart, but is golden and soft when you get to it. Dan Lepard, their bread guru, asked me to mention 'something sweet about Gail Stephens [the shop's founder and owner]. It is a very special bakery and we are proud of what we have created.' I am gradually working my way through their tarts, cakes and the traiteur department, and this is the recipe Dan developed at Alastair Little's restaurant, after a story told him by a French pâtissier. 'The stone of a soft fruit contains not just the heart of the flavour, but also the knowledge of the plant that bore it. It is essential to use a stone when cooking any fruit. Possibly a romantic notion, but I believed it.' The apricots stand proud in this tart, with beautifully singed tips.

Serves 8
16 firm blush apricots
200g/7oz rich puff pastry
50g/scant 2oz soft-set
    apricot preserve

Frangipane
240g/8oz ground almonds,
    plus the kernels from
    3 of the apricots
150g/5oz caster sugar
200g/7oz unsalted butter,
    softened
3 organic eggs
100g/3½oz plain flour

Preheat the oven to 180°C/350°F/Gas 4.

Halve the apricots with a small, sharp knife, and remove the stones. Crack three of the stones with a hammer to extract the kernels.

For the frangipane, place the almonds, apricot kernels and sugar in a food processor and process until the kernels have blended with the sugar and almonds. Next add the butter and mix until pale and smooth. Beat in the eggs, one by one, then finally lightly beat in the flour. Transfer the mixture to a small container and leave in a cool place while preparing the pastry.

Roll out the pastry into a thin circle large enough to cover and overlap the sides of a 25cm/10 inch tart ring. Place the ring on a baking sheet lined with greaseproof paper. Gently press the pastry down into the ring, and prick the base of the pastry lightly with a fork. Put the pastry in the fridge to chill for 10–15 minutes.

Spread the frangipane over the base of the tart, then sit the apricot halves upright in the frangipane. Place the tart in the centre of the oven and bake for 15 minutes. Reduce the heat to 160°C/325°F/Gas 3 and continue baking for 35–45 minutes, until the pastry is crisp and the frangipane light brown in colour. Warm the apricot preserve in a saucepan over a low heat, with a little water to make a syrup, and brush this over the tart. Turn out and serve warm with crème fraîche.

CHOCOLATE AND APRICOT TART

It was September last year when Neale Whitaker sent me to Jerez to write about sherry for Food Illustrated *with Mark Sainsbury and chef Sam Clark, two of the co-owners of Moro. We had an amazing four days, and an even more amazing four nights, culminating in the all-night flamenco in the Buleria to celebrate the grape harvest. We worshipped at the shrine that Sam and Mark had wanted to visit — the bodega of Miguel Valdespino, one of the last of the family-run sherry-making businesses — and spent hours drinking his sherries and appraising his sherry vinegars. We also ate seafood like I have never eaten, from at least nine kinds of prawns to unknown delights like 'ventresca' — belly of tuna — and sea anemones that we'd seen arrive minutes before in a fisherman's boat. A nine-course dinner at Miguel's brother's restaurant La Mesa Rodonda combined the strong flavours of southern Spain with the delicate spicing of North Africa. On our return we vowed to have a reunion, so we met up at Moro in Clerkenwell. We followed delicious tapas and Valdespino sherry with briks of crab, and partridge, and then I couldn't resist their chocolate and apricot tart. They make it with a dense, tart apricot paste which is sold in Iranian shops in long, flat strips. If you can't find this, use apricot jam instead, with a little lemon juice. It is important that the apricot layer is slightly tart so that it cuts through the rich chocolate.*

Serves 8–10
225g/7½oz plain flour
75g/2½oz icing sugar
150g/5oz unsalted butter
2 egg yolks

Filling
125g/4½oz apricot paste,
   or apricot jam mixed with
   the juice of ½ a lemon
180g/6oz unsalted butter
200g/7oz plain chocolate
4 eggs
125g/4½oz caster sugar

Make the pastry in a food processor: combine the flour, icing sugar and butter until evenly blended. Add the egg yolks and continue to blend until the ingredients come together. Wrap in cling film and put in the fridge for half an hour. Preheat the oven to 200°C/400°F/Gas 6. Roll out the pastry and line a 30cm/12 inch tart tin. Bake blind for 15 minutes, then remove the beans, prick the base with a fork, and return to the oven for 5 minutes. Turn the heat down to 180°C/350°F/Gas 4.

To make the filling: if you are using apricot paste, melt it in a saucepan with a little water, then spread it over the base of the tart. Alternatively, spread over a thin layer of the apricot jam. Melt the butter and chocolate together in a double saucepan. Whisk the eggs and sugar together until they are pale and light. Gently fold the chocolate mixture into the eggs and sugar. Transfer to the tart shell, and even out with the back of a spoon. Bake for 20 minutes, or until the chocolate has formed a slight crust. Leave to cool slightly, then turn out and serve with yoghurt or crème fraîche.

SIMON HOPKINSON'S CHOCOLATE TART

If there is a heaven, this is it. I speak as a hopeless chocoholic, not that I am remotely interested in weaning myself off the stuff. We had briefly corresponded, and Simon had kindly agreed to my using any of his recipes I wanted to; this one is from his book Roast Chicken and Other Stories, *which I go back to time and time again, not that I ever leave it for very long in between whiles. After all, there are things in it like this chocolate tart, which rates as one of the mega culinary experiences of all time.*

If anyone is insane enough to believe they can do better, I want to hear about it. The only tinkering I have ever done is to make a cocoa pastry with Green and Black's organic cocoa, but the original way is unparalleled.

Serves 8
180g/6oz butter
75g/2½oz icing sugar
2 egg yolks
225g/8oz plain flour

Filling
2 eggs
3 egg yolks
45g/1½oz caster sugar
150g/5oz unsalted butter
200g/7oz best bitter
   chocolate, broken
   into pieces

To make the pastry, put the butter, icing sugar and egg yolks in a bowl or food processor and work together quickly. Blend in the flour, and work to a homogeneous paste. Chill for at least 1 hour.

Preheat the oven to 180°C/350°F/Gas 4. Roll out the pastry as thinly as you can, and line a 25cm/10 inch tart tin. Bake blind for about 25 minutes, or until pale biscuit coloured, but thoroughly cooked through. Remove from the oven and increase the temperature to 190°C/375°F/Gas 5.

To make the filling, put the eggs, yolks and caster sugar in a bowl and beat vigorously together, preferably with an electric whisk, until really thick and fluffy. Melt the butter and chocolate together in a bowl over a saucepan of barely simmering water, stirring until smooth. Pour on to the egg mixture while just warm. Briefly beat together until well amalgamated, then pour into the pastry case. Return to the hot oven for 5 minutes, then remove and leave to cool. Serve with thick cream.

SALLY CLARKE'S PRUNE TART

I have always admired Sally Clarke's food. Dinner at her Kensington Church Street restaurant is one menu, with no choice, unless you happen not to like one of the dishes. You have to be very good to get away with it, and she is. So often I have languished over long menus, utterly unable to make a decision. If you go to her restaurant you have taken away the burden of choice; it is like going to a friend's for dinner and speculating excitedly on what she's cooked. In her next-door shop there is a café, breads, cakes, cheeses, vegetables and cream of the absolute best, and her eponymous chocolate truffles, which are the last word in temptation.

The other day I was having lunch in the café with a friend; I had a divine slice of chocolate cake, but his prune tart was diviner. I came home and faxed Sally for the recipe, and here it is.

Serves 8
120g/4oz butter
50g/scant 2oz icing sugar
2 small egg yolks
180g/6oz plain flour

Filling
12 pitted prunes
a little tea, cognac and
    orange juice
1 egg and 2 egg yolks
80g/scant 3oz caster sugar
pure vanilla essence, or the
    scraped-out contents of
    1 vanilla pod
300ml/10fl oz double cream
75ml/2½fl oz milk

Soak the prunes overnight in a splash each of tea, cognac and orange juice.

To make the pastry, put the butter, icing sugar and egg yolks in a bowl or food processor and work together quickly. Blend in the flour, and work to a homogeneous paste. Chill for at least 1 hour.

Preheat the oven to 180°C/350°F/Gas 4. Roll out the pastry thinly and line a 22cm/9 inch tart tin. Bake blind for about 25 minutes, or until crisp and golden. Remove from the oven and turn the heat down to 150°C/300°F/Gas 2.

For the filling, beat the egg and yolks with the sugar and vanilla until smooth. Heat the cream and milk together until hot, and pour over the egg mixture. Strain and leave on one side to cool slightly.

Place the prunes in the tart shell and pour over the custard. Bake for 20–25 minutes or until lightly set. Serve cool, with whipped cream.

FIG TART WITH TOBACCO SYRUP

The Sunday AA Gill wrote about Richard Corrigan at The Lindsay House is indelibly printed on my brain. I knew and loved Richard's food already, but hadn't yet been to the new restaurant, and when I read about this pudding I couldn't stop laughing. I had to try it. I was due to go out to my birthday lunch with my great friend Janie on the Monday. She had already booked somewhere else. As I left Somerset that morning, I called her. I didn't have to say anything. She merely informed me that she'd changed the booking to Lindsay House, but that it had taken her an hour and a half to get through!

So we went, had the best lunch we'd had all year, and then ordered the pudding. In a curious way the gingery innards of the fig, when they dry out a little, are not unlike tobacco, and the subtlety with which my favourite Irish chef used it silenced any thought of novelty for novelty's sake. Go to the restaurant whether the tart is on the menu or not. Nobody cooks the more spurned carnivorous delights like pigs' trotters, sweetbreads, pigs' ears and tongue like Richard, who brines and cures all his own meat in his subterranean kitchen. And I think he makes the best mashed potato I know, which arrives at the table in little steaming copper saucepans. He has recently won his first Michelin star. There should be a second.

Makes 6 individual tarts
240g/8oz puff pastry
6–8 ripe figs
30g/1oz unsalted butter,
    melted

Frangipane
30g/1oz caster sugar
15g/½oz ground almonds
½ tsp cornflour
30g/1oz unsalted butter

Tobacco syrup
180g/6oz sugar
150ml/5fl oz water
2 tsp pipe tobacco
a pinch of cornflour

Preheat the oven to 200°C/400°F/Gas 6.

Roll out the pastry and cut out six 10cm/4 inch circles. Make the frangipane by mixing all the ingredients together until smooth. Spread a bit of it on to each pastry circle. Thinly slice the figs and arrange in a circular fashion on top of the frangipane. Brush the tops with melted butter and bake for 12–15 minutes.

For the syrup, bring the sugar and water to the boil, then turn off the heat and infuse the tobacco in the liquid for 10 seconds before straining the syrup through a sieve. Dissolve the cornflour in about a teaspoon of cold water, and then blend it into the syrup. Drizzle a little around each fig tart on its plate, and serve.

Banana Tart

Another fantastic recipe from the talented Mr Corrigan. He serves his with raisin syrup and rum cream. I just handed round some home-made cold crème anglaise which had graced the previous night's pudding, but a little snifter of dark rum and brown sugar beaten into some good thick cream would be delicious.

Serves 8

500g/just over 1lb puff
    pastry
8 ripe but firm small
    bananas – over-ripe will
    cook to cotton wool
a knob of unsalted butter,
    melted
icing sugar

Frangipane

100g/3½oz unsalted butter,
    softened
100g/3½oz caster sugar
1 egg and 1 egg yolk, beaten
100g/3½oz ground almonds
20g/⅔oz plain flour

Roll out the pastry and cut out eight 10cm/4 inch squares or 12cm/5 inch discs. Place them on a baking sheet lined with baking parchment. With the back of a knife blade, draw a rim just inside each disc and prick the centre with a fork. Chill in the fridge for at least 30 minutes. Preheat the oven to 200°C/400°F/Gas 6.

For the frangipane, cream the butter and sugar with an electric whisk until pale and fluffy. Add the beaten egg and yolk, then the almonds and flour, beating all the while. Spoon the mixture into the middle of each pastry disc, leaving the rims clear and enough space for a band of sliced bananas to surround the frangipane. Slice the bananas and fan the slices around the frangipane, closely overlapping, then top the frangipane with the remaining slices. Brush with melted butter, then finish with a fine dusting of sifted icing sugar. Bake for about 20 minutes, until the bananas are caramelized and shiny and the pastry puffed up and golden. Domestic ovens are not always good at caramelizing, but you can always brûlee the banana tops with a bit more icing sugar and a blowtorch when they come out of the oven. Serve hot.

RHUBARB MERINGUE PIE

When Nigella Lawson's book How to Eat, The Pleasures and Principles of Good Food *came out, a lot of serious cookery book junkies, myself very much included, breathed a sigh of relief. The preponderance of celebrity chef's books, with restaurant recipes, had left us feeling inadequate, exhausted, hungry for sheer simplicity, but the best. And not just for another 'How To' manual. Some of us are also looking for brilliant writing and a distinctive style, not a professional's dishes ghosted into a prose style that is clearly not the author's voice. Well, Nigella's had it all. She also gave credit for all the recipes she'd snitched from others. Where things come from I find fascinating, as fascinating as what they've been transmuted into.*

We met when I went to interview her for Food Illustrated, *and became friends as a result. And 'allies', as Nigella wrote when inscribing my copy of her book. This is the recipe she wanted me to include, which she dedicates, in her book, to her sister Horatia. It is utterly delicious, and not just as a tart. I have lots of rhubarb left when I've cooked it for a jelly, so I make a rhubarb meringue pudding out of the top two-thirds of this recipe, omitting the pastry.*

Serves 6

800g/just under 2lb rhubarb, untrimmed weight
juice of ½ an orange
2 eggs, separated
150g/5oz plus 120g/4oz caster sugar
2 tbsp plain flour
30g/1oz unsalted butter, melted
¼ tsp cream of tartar

Make shortcrust pastry (page 139) with 120g/4oz flour, using orange juice instead of water to make it cohere. Chill, then line a 22cm/9 inch tart tin. Preheat the oven to 200°C/400°F/Gas 6. Bake the pastry blind for 20 minutes. Remove from the oven and brush the pastry with beaten egg white, then leave to cool.

Trim the rhubarb and chop it into roughly 1cm/½ inch slices. Put it in a saucepan with the orange juice and heat briefly, just until the rawness is taken off it. Remove, drain, and keep the liquid.

Beat the egg yolks in a small bowl. In another bowl, mix 150g/5oz sugar with the flour and the melted butter. Then add the yolks and enough of the rhubarb liquid to turn it into a smooth, runny paste. Put the rhubarb into the pastry case and pour the mixture over it. Bake until just set, 20–30 minutes.

Beat the egg whites until they form soft peaks, add 60g/2oz sugar, and continue to beat until glossy. Then fold in the remaining sugar and the cream of tartar, using a metal spoon. Spoon this over the baked tart to completely cover the fruit, sprinkle with a bit more caster sugar, and return to the oven for about 15 minutes, until the peaks are bronze-tipped. Nigella likes to eat it cold, but says that for most tastes, 10–12 minutes out of the oven is about right.

Mjuk Toscakaka

Kristina von Wrede is an exceptionally talented home cook. She is Swedish, and lives near me in Somerset, and I know whenever I go to dinner with her and her husband Fritz that the food will be original and unlike anything else anybody I know would cook. Organic vegetables and herbs from her walled kitchen garden, her own geese, and wonderful wild boar and venison in the autumn from Fritz's family in Westphalia.

I spent a morning there recently, with Kristina making the following three tarts while I watched and took notes. 'The Swedes still do a lot of baking even though they've got jobs,' Kristina informed me. 'And the quality of their flour is very good.' Her kitchen constantly smells of baking, home-made breads, cakes, little caraway-seeded rolls, pizzas, a lot of the ingredients brought back from London's Swedish deli Swedish Affar, or from Ikea.

'This tart is very simple but very effective,' Kristina says. 'That's what I like about Swedish food. In the old days, a good housewife had to be able to bake seven kinds of biscuit before she married. Because the Swedish are still very much a farming people – it was 90 per cent in the last century – and it is such a big country, they are very particular with their baking. They can't just go down to a local shop.'

Serves 6 – 8
150g/5oz butter
125g/4oz caster sugar
2 eggs
1 tsp vanilla extract
150g/5oz plain flour
1 tsp baking powder
5 tbsp water

For the top
30g/1oz flaked almonds
60g/2oz butter
5 tbsp caster sugar
1 tbsp plain flour
1 tbsp milk

Preheat the oven to 180°C/350°F/Gas 4 and butter a 22cm/9 inch tart tin.

Cream the butter and sugar together thoroughly in a bowl. Beat in the eggs, little by little, then add the vanilla extract. Sift in the flour and baking powder, beat thoroughly, then add the water and continue beating until smooth. Scrape into the buttered tart tin, smooth the top, and bake for about 30 minutes. Remove from the oven, and turn the temperature up to 200°C/400°F/Gas 6.

For the top, put all the ingredients together into a saucepan and heat. Allow to bubble to amalgamate the mixture, then spoon this over the tart and return to the oven to brown for 5 minutes. Don't let it burn. You will have a deliciously fudgy, crunchy top. Serve plain, without cream, warm or cold.

MJUK MANDELTARTA
SOFT ALMOND TART

There is a delicious organic Dutch marzipan that you can buy from health food shops; get it if you can, some of the more commercial makes are deeply inferior. Or you could make your own.

Serves 8

300g/10oz organic marzipan

grated zest and juice
of 1 orange

3 eggs

2 tbsp plain flour

generous ½ tsp baking
powder

Preheat the oven to 180°C/350°F/Gas 4 and butter a 25cm/10 inch springform tart tin.

Add the marzipan to the grated orange zest in a bowl, then beat in the eggs. You are aiming for a smooth, unlumpy dough. Add the orange juice and beat with a whisk. Sift the flour and baking powder over the mixture and whisk again. Turn the mixture into the buttered tin and bake in the lower third of the oven for 30 – 40 minutes.

If it rises well, slice it in half and fill it with crème pâtissière, or lemon or orange curd. Otherwise, spread one of these over the top. If you've done the former, you could sift icing sugar over the top, but if you want a more special tart, spread the top with whipped cream and then add some soft fruit — raspberries, loganberries, blackcurrants. Kristina defrosts her own soft fruits if she is making this in the winter, making sure that the juice is properly drained first. Sometimes she adds melted chocolate to the whipped cream, and some finely chopped crystallized orange.

Ambrosia Kaka

This is like the Toscakaka (see page 80), but made with the zest and juice of an orange instead of with water, and topped with an orangey glaze.

Serves 6 – 8
150g/5oz slightly salted
    butter
125g/4oz caster sugar
2 eggs
150g/5oz plain flour
1½ tsp baking powder
grated zest and juice
    of 1 orange

'Vanilkram' filling (optional)

2 yolks
5 tbsp each of double cream
    and milk
1 tbsp potato flour,
    or 1½ tbsp cornflour
1 tbsp caster sugar
½ a split vanilla pod,
    the middle scraped out

For the top

7½ tbsp icing sugar
1½ tbsp orange juice
3 small pieces of crystallized
    orange, cut into tiny cubes

Preheat the oven to 180°C/350°F/Gas 4 and butter a 22cm/9 inch tart tin.

Cream the butter and sugar together thoroughly in a bowl, then add the eggs, one at a time, beating together thoroughly. Sift in the flour and baking powder, beat well, then add the orange zest and 5 tablespoons of juice, and continue beating until smooth. Scrape into the buttered tart tin and bake for 30–40 minutes.

For the *vanilkram*, whisk everything together in a saucepan, stirring over a gentle heat until thickened. Remove the vanilla pod and leave to cool.

Once you have removed the tart from the oven, leave it to cool for 15 minutes. Halve it if you like, and fill with *vanilkram*.

For the top, mix together the icing sugar and orange juice, then spread over the tart, and sprinkle with the crystallized fruit. The result should be a thin glaze, not a thick one.

SWEET TARTS

"This most versatile and perfectly self-contained of foods is without doubt one of the great joys of my cooking life, equally as pleasurable in the making as in the eating."

Roast Fig and Honey Tart with Cointreau (page 112)

PEACH, VANILLA AND AMARETTI TARTE TATIN

Invention in the culinary world is a difficult and risky thing to define. We are all influenced by so many people, and there is no knowing, when one comes up with something one imagines to be original, whether or not someone else hasn't thought of it first – it is more than likely that they have. I am under no illusions about that. However, when I first dreamt up this tart I have to confess I felt really proud of it, and amazed that, first time round, it tasted quite as good as it did. The amber-hued peaches speckled with vanilla and sticky with caramel, and the pastry, not overpowered, but brought to life with crushed amaretti, make it something where all the contrasting flavours complement and add, yet the three very different notes remain simple, true. Try it and see.

Serves 8

For the pastry

8 amaretti
180g/6oz plain flour, sifted
90g/3oz unsalted butter,
    cut into pieces
2–3 tbsp iced water

For the top

8 ripe peaches (white are
    the absolute best, but
    yellow-fleshed are fine)
juice of 1 lemon
1 vanilla pod
90g/3oz caster sugar
60g/2oz unsalted butter

To make the pastry, crush the amaretti in a food processor, add the flour and butter and process briefly to combine, then add 2–3 tablespoons iced water and process until the mixture comes together. Wrap in greaseproof paper and chill for at least 20 minutes.

Preheat the oven to 190°C/375°F/Gas 5. Roll out the pastry to 1cm/½ inch more than the circumference of the pan – I use a heavy, 25cm/10 inch diameter Cousances enamelled cast-iron frying pan with a metal handle that I can put in the oven – and set the pastry to one side.

Scald the peaches in boiling water for 30 seconds. Peel, and sprinkle them with lemon juice to prevent discolouration.

Split the vanilla pod and scrape it out into the sugar. Warm the sugar in the frying pan until it is a deep, dark brown and totally liquid. Do not stir, but move the pan around to prevent burning. Remove from the heat and dot with half of the butter. Put half a peach in the middle of the sugar mixture, cut side up. Quarter the rest, and, starting at the outside of the pan, lay them next to each other in a tightly packed wheel. Arrange the remaining quarters in an inside wheel. Dot with the rest of the butter and put the pan back over the heat for 2–3 minutes to gently start the cooking.

Remove from the heat, cover with a mantle of pastry that you tuck inside the pan edge, and bake for 25–30 minutes. Remove from the oven and leave for 10 minutes before inverting on to a plate. Delicious with crème fraîche.

PEAR AND GINGER TARTE TATIN

It is the beginning of November. The first smallish and deceptively bullet-like Conference pears are in the shops, the forecast is for storm force winds and floods. And I've got George Morley and her husband Shawn Whiteside and baby Charlie coming to stay. (See her Leek Tart recipe on page 61.) George is being the perfect weekend guest and bringing down Friday night's supper from London. I have a sort of sixth sense that it might be worth making a pudding. Other than seven pears, my storecupboard shrieks ginger in syrup. Ginger is the great warming herb of Chinese medicine, and feels like the most eligible partner for the cool scentedness of the pears. Turn back to the previous page if you need confidence-bolstering to attempt a tarte tatin; it really, really isn't difficult, any more than a soufflé is, although it is always held up to be.

Serves 8

7 pears

juice of 1 lemon

80g/nearly 3oz vanilla
   caster sugar

60g/2oz unsalted butter

2–3 tbsp ginger syrup and
   3 knobs of ginger, cut into
   small dice

Make shortcrust pastry (page 139) with 180g/6oz flour and 90g/3oz unsalted butter, and chill. Preheat the oven to 180°C/350°F/Gas 4 and put a baking sheet in to heat. Roll out the pastry to 1cm/½ inch more than the circumference of the pan; I use my 25cm/10 inch cast-iron frying pan that I can put in the oven. Peel, core and halve the pears; turn them in lemon juice to prevent discolouration.

Warm the sugar in the frying pan until it liquifies. The moment the sugar is treacly brown all over but not burnt, remove it from the heat and dot with half the butter; it will bubble up and become absorbed. Then pour over some ginger syrup, a couple of tablespoons or three; any more will be intrusive. Fit the pears head to tail in spokes, sardine style, around the pan. Or, halve the halves vertically into quarters and tuck them on their sides, then cut circular shapes to fill the gaps in the middle, core side up. Sprinkle the ginger pieces over the pears, and then cover the whole in a blanket of pastry, tucking it in under the pears around the edges.

Bake on the middle shelf of the oven on the preheated baking sheet for about 30 minutes. The juices should be bubbling stickily away around the edge. Remove from the oven and leave to cool for about 10 minutes before inverting on to a plate. The mahogany-tinted pears that gaze up at you should be perfectly cooked and glossily glazed with caramel.

Pass round thick cream, and a bottle of eau de vie de poires if you are lucky enough to have any, and feel the ginger's warming presence as it hits your insides.

A Tatin of Apricots stuffed with Almond Paste

January, and the memory of summer fruits is just that. When Miranda brought home two Australian girls, over for a schools' hockey tour, I was determined that they should get something to eat that wasn't entirely sunshine free. Alighting on a box of apricots, I decided to fill them with a rich frangipane paste, and bake them under a tatin crust.

Serves 8
30g/1oz ground almonds
30g/1oz unsalted butter, cut into small pieces
30g/1oz vanilla caster sugar
1 egg
a few drops of bitter almond essence (I use Culpeper's)
2–3 dozen fresh apricots
90g/3oz caster sugar

Make shortcrust pastry (page 139) with 180g/6oz flour and 90g/3oz unsalted butter, and chill. Preheat the oven to 180°C/350°F/Gas 4 and roll out the pastry to 1 cm/½ inch more than the circumference of a large ovenproof frying pan.

Mix the ground almonds, butter and vanilla sugar with the egg and a few drops of almond essence to make a rich paste. Slice each apricot in half and remove the stones, then fill the cut halves with the paste.

Warm the caster sugar in the ovenproof pan in which the tart is to be cooked. When it caramelizes, remove from the heat and pack the apricots tightly into the pan, paste side up, in circles, with any left over in a double layer at the centre. Cover with a blanket of pastry, tucking it in around the edges of the apricots, and bake for 35 minutes. Leave it to rest for 10 minutes before inverting on to a plate. Serve with crème fraîche.

Lemon Meringue Pie

This is another of those golden age of childhood recipes, and one of the first puddings I learned to cook. My grandmother's cook, Rhoda, steely grey hair in a taut bun, and maroon flowered dress worn nearly down to her black old maid's shoes, had the lightest touch that pastry ever saw. She always made this when my brother Daniel and I went to stay at Upper Parrock, our grandparents' beautiful mediaeval hilltop house in East Sussex. And she always judged it right. The gloopy lemon filling was never too sweet, never too cornfloured, and the top rose cloud-like, stepped, a breath of weightless meringue with that final, brittle brown top that a spoon had to crunch through before meeting the gooey middle and the smooth, tart lemon. The addition of a few crushed cardamom seeds to the lemon filling robs the pudding of its nursery status, but is well worth the experimentation.

Serves 6
22cm/9 inch shortcrust
    pastry case, chilled
    (page 139)
beaten egg white, for brushing

Lemon filling
grated zest and juice of 3
    organic lemons
45g/1½oz cornflour
300ml/10fl oz water
3 large egg yolks
80g/2¾oz vanilla caster
    sugar
60g/2oz unsalted butter,
    cut into small pieces

Meringue
3 large egg whites
120g/4oz vanilla caster
    sugar

Preheat the oven to 190°C/375°F/Gas 5. Bake the pastry blind for 15 minutes, then remove the beans, brush the pastry with beaten egg white, and return to the oven for 5 minutes. Remove the pastry case from the oven and turn the heat down to 180°C/350°F/Gas 4.

For the filling, put the lemon zest and juice in the top of a double boiler. Add the cornflour and whisk in with 2 tablespoons of the water until you have a smooth paste. Bring the remaining water to the boil, add to the lemon mixture and keep whisking over simmering water until the mixture is thick and bubbling. Remove from the heat and whisk in the egg yolks, sugar and butter. Leave to cool slightly while you make the meringue.

Whisk the egg whites until stiff, scatter in one-third of the sugar, and whisk again until stiff. Fold in another third of the sugar with a metal spoon. Spread the lemon mixture over the pastry. Pile the meringue on top and sprinkle it with the remaining sugar. Bake for 15–20 minutes. Allow to cool slightly, then turn out. Best served with thin cream.

SEVILLE ORANGE AND MARMALADE TART

This is a delicious winter pudding for the Seville orange season, or, out of season, you can make it with less sugar, ordinary oranges and a lemon, or blood oranges if you want an unguessable-looking tart. I once made a blood orange and cardamom ice cream to accompany it, which was pink, fragrant and utterly delicious. Perfect after a rich goose, which I always cook on New Year's Eve.

Serves 6 – 8
22cm/9 inch shortcrust
  pastry case, chilled
  (page 139)
beaten egg white, for brushing
2 – 3 tbsp tart orange
  marmalade
grated zest and juice of
  4 Seville oranges
120g/4oz unsalted butter,
  softened
225g/7½oz vanilla caster
  sugar
4 large eggs, beaten

Preheat the oven to 190°C/375°F/Gas 5. Bake the pastry blind for 15 minutes, then remove the beans, prick the base with a fork, brush with beaten egg white, and cook for a further 5 minutes. Remove the pastry from the oven and turn the heat down to 180°C/350°F/Gas 4.

Spread the marmalade over the bottom of the pastry case. Put the grated orange zest in a bowl. Beat in the butter and sugar, then add the beaten eggs and whisk everything together. Place the bowl over a saucepan of simmering water and stir until the sugar has dissolved. Remove from the heat and stir in the orange juice. Pour into the marmalade-lined pastry case and return to the oven for 20 minutes or so, until barely set. Serve warm, with thick cream.

RICOTTA TART WITH RUM-SOAKED SULTANAS

This is surprisingly un-rich, the liquor-soaked sultanas adding a mellow sharpness, the whisked egg whites a soufflé-like lightness that the children adored. It is phenomenally quick to make, and it cooked while they were tucking into their lasagne. I added chocolate to their tart, turning it into a swirly, marble-topped picture; the grown-ups' one I left plain. Leave the tarts for 15 minutes before turning them out.

Serves 6—8

22cm/9 inch shortcrust
  pastry case, chilled
  (page 139)
2 tbsp dark rum
60g/2oz sultanas
2 x 250g/8oz pots of ricotta,
  or 500g/just over 1lb
  fresh ricotta if you can
  find it
5 eggs, 4 of them separated
3 tbsp potato flour
90g/3oz vanilla caster sugar
1 orange or lemon
60g/2oz best bitter
  chocolate and the same of
  unsalted butter (optional)

Preheat the oven to 190°C/375°F/Gas 5. Bake the pastry blind for 15 minutes, then remove the beans and bake for a further 5 minutes. Leave to cool, and turn the oven down to 180°C/350°F/Gas 4.

Heat the rum gently in a small saucepan with the sultanas and allow them to absorb the liquor. Push the ricotta through a sieve or the smallest holes of a mouli into a large bowl, add the whole egg and four yolks, and mix thoroughly. Add the potato flour and vanilla sugar. Pour the rum-soaked sultanas into the ricotta mixture and incorporate. Grate in the citrus zest. Whisk the egg whites until stiff, stir 1 tablespoon into the ricotta mixture, and then lightly fold in the rest. If you are doing the plain version, stop here, and spoon the mixture into your pastry case.

If you are doing the chocolate version, melt the chocolate and butter together over a very low heat, then pour lightly over the top of the ricotta mixture. Pour the mixture into the pastry case, minimally disturbing the chocolate into marbled swirls with a skewer.

Bake for 45—50 minutes — it should be set right across, but not rigidly so. Leave to sink and cool, and turn out after about 20 minutes. I think it should be eaten cold, or at most with a bare memory of warmth.

"The first June strawberries, when not devoured straight from the punnet, are christened in a tart with a voluptuous, vanilla-ey crème pâtissière, in which they have been plunged waist deep, and glazed to gloopy perfection."

Strawberry Tart

This is the spirit of summer; the first June strawberries from nearby Cheddar, when not devoured straight from the punnet, are christened in a tart with a voluptuous vanilla-ey crème pâtissière, in which they have been plunged waist deep and glazed to gloopy perfection. I cannot understand why anyone could be fearful of making this look as good as one from the finest French pâtissier. It is nuts and bolts cookery. If you can make pastry, the rest's a breeze. If you can't, either learn how to from the pastry section of this book, or, better still, from watching someone who can, or give this book to someone who'll use it.

All three of my children put it on their top three pudding list, and I think I agree. I confess I always make a hubcap-sized version rather than the normal tart-sized one. This is not because I only make it when people are coming over to lunch or supper, it is because everybody in my family eats gargantuan slices of it, and if there is any left, it is whittled sneakily away on the day. This is not a tart to be served up the following day, tiredly, pinkily soggy; it simply doesn't work. Just eat lots of it.

Serves 8 greedy people
about 1kg/2lb strawberries
about 4 tbsp redcurrant jelly

Crème pâtissière
375ml/13fl oz Jersey
    or full fat milk
1 vanilla pod, split
4 egg yolks
120g/4oz caster sugar
50g/just under 2oz cornflour

Make a pâte sucrée (page 140) with 180g/6oz white flour, 90g/3oz unsalted butter, 2 dessertspoons icing sugar, 2 egg yolks and a little ice-cold water; chill for at least an hour. Preheat the oven to 200°C/400°F/Gas 6. Line a 30cm/ 12 inch tart tin with the pastry and bake blind, then remove the beans and return to the oven for 10–15 minutes, until golden and cooked. Watch closely: the edges burn swiftly, and you don't want scorch marks on the bottom. Leave to cool.

For the crème pâtissière, scald the milk with the vanilla pod and its scraped-out seeds. Whisk the egg yolks, sugar and cornflour together in a bowl, then pour the hot milk on to them and continue whisking. Remove the vanilla pod. Return the mixture to the saucepan and stir over a gentle heat until thickened. Turn into a bowl and cool, whisking every so often. When cold, scrape into the pastry case with a rubber spatula. Turn the tart out on to a plate or bread board.

Hull the strawberries. Starting at the edge of the tart, stick them upright into the crème pâtissière in a circle and work your way in, using smaller strawberries for each circle. Melt the redcurrant jelly with a tablespoon of water, then brush it liberally over the strawberries and the custardy gaps. Stand back and admire before you cut it.

Sugar-Topped Raspberry Plate Tart

By late Lenten March, it's time to cast puritanism aside, and I succumb to unseasonal soft fruit if it's to be found. Raspberries and blueberries this weekend, the former from Spain, so I got to work with a sharp raspberry tart with a last-minute flood of whisked cream and duck egg yolk funnelled into it. I don't know whether there is a consensus as to when a tart becomes a pie, but I think depth is probably the key to it, not crust. This tart has a lid on it, a delicious, brittle, crackly sugar crust of pastry sprinkled with demerara, but it is not deep enough to transmogrify into a pie, it is a plate tart. Utterly simple to make, and oozing a confluence of raspberry and ivory juices. If you can bear to wait until June, you can use English raspberries, but I couldn't resist this dress rehearsal.

Serves 6
500g/a little over 1lb
    raspberries
100g/generous 3oz vanilla
    caster sugar
1 egg, separated
about 2 tbsp demerara sugar
200ml/7fl oz double cream

Make shortcrust pastry (page 139) with 300g/10oz organic plain flour and 150g/5oz unsalted butter, and chill. Roll out and use half the pastry to line the bottom of a pie plate or shallow, earthenware dish, about 22cm/9 inches in diameter. Preheat the oven to 190°C/375°F/Gas 5.

Scatter the raspberries over the pastry with the vanilla sugar. Put the remaining pastry on top, crimp the edges with a fork to seal, and brush with lightly beaten egg white. Sprinkle with a thin film of sugar, demerara for real crunch, and cut a cross centrally through the pastry lid to let the steam escape. Bake for about 40 minutes.

Do not be alarmed when you see how pallid the crust is; it is not yolked, it is whited. Whisk the cream together with the egg yolk – I had a duck egg – and very gently and slowly pour the mixture through a small funnel down into the hole. This is the only difficult bit; you don't want a flooded crust. Then return the tart to the oven for 10 minutes. Eat warm or hot; you will not need extra cream.

Brûléed Blackcurrant or Blueberry Tart

This is a real show-off of a tart, which I started making when my children gave me a blow-torch for Christmas one year. It is still a fantastic thrill aiming a jet of blue flame at the sugary surface and watching the beaded brown bubbles form, crystallize, and turn into a caramelized mahogany sheet. It is just as much of a thrill to crack it, like an egg, with the back of a spoon, and eat the splintery shards of sugar with the strong, tart blackcurrants. If you use blueberries, the cinnamon works equally as well, the result is just milder to the palate, as you would expect.

Serves 6
300g/10oz blackcurrants
    or blueberries
a pinch of ground cinnamon
a little light muscovado sugar
2 large eggs
2 egg yolks
250ml/8fl oz double cream
4 tbsp Kirsch
about 3 tbsp granulated
    sugar

Make shortcrust pastry (page 139) with 120g/4oz flour and 60g/2oz butter, adding 1 tablespoon caster sugar to sweeten it. Chill, then roll out and line a 22cm/9 inch tart tin. Preheat the oven to 190°C/375°F/Gas 5. Bake the pastry blind for 10 minutes, then remove the beans and bake for a further 10 minutes. Remove the pastry from the oven and turn the heat down to 180°C/350°F/Gas 4.

Put the fruit in a saucepan with 2 tablespoons of water and a pinch of cinnamon, and simmer very briefly. Sweeten to taste with light muscovado sugar. In a bowl, beat together the eggs, yolks, cream and Kirsch, and add a little more sugar to taste. Place a single layer of fruit in the pastry case, then pour in the cream mixture and return to the oven for about 30 minutes, until just firm but with a slightly 'sad' centre. Leave to cool.

Just before you want to serve it, strew a thin layer of granulated sugar over the tart. If you don't have a blowtorch and are going to perform this feat under the grill, cover the pastry edges with a strip of foil, then blast the tart until the sugar bubbles and caramelizes. The thin, burnt brown skating rink top marries beautifully with the creamy, fruity middle.

APPLE TARTS

Apples and pastry. Short, buttery, tart, sugary, the apple tart is one of the greats, has endured changing fashions and seasons, and is as comfortable at the simplest as at the grandest of occasions. A perfect French apple tart, with regiments of fanned, sliced apples, gooey yet slightly burnt-edged, with a gloss of sieved apricot jam. A glossy, bronzed tarte Tatin, dripping caramelized sugar, with a plop of crème fraîche and Calvados. A creamy tart with thick slices of fried apple nestling in the pastry, anointed with egg yolks, cinnamon and cream.

Even now, in gloomy February, I have still got a few sharp-scented cooking apples from one of my trees lurking unsullied in a box, rubbing shoulders with one or two blackened neighbours. Paired with some organic Golden Delicious, which I deign to cook with but not to eat raw, or cooked down and puréed with brown sugar, butter, orange zest and juice, the apple helps transform this storecupboard month into something more living, less preserved.

This weekend I placed an unevenly rolled oblong of Baker & Spice puff pastry (see page 141) on a floured baking sheet, scoring a rim about 2cm/an inch or so from the outside edge. Then, leaving the rim clear, I laid peeled, quartered, finely sliced and overlapping Golden Delicious all the way round, and plonked two punnets of blueberries in the middle in a generous layer. Scattered with sugar, dotted with butter, it was cooked for 10 minutes before I poured a layer of peach jam, melted with a bit of water, but not sieved, over the fruit, returning it to the oven for 10 minutes.

We ate the sugary slices in our hands, crisply crusted edges, slightly sogged middles, with the thickened, purply juices bleeding into the apple edges. A recipe? Not quite, but a pudding very definitely, lightly, fruitily satisfying, with no need of cream or spoons. The following recipes are all variations on the apple tart, some minimal, some maximal, but all are a delicious end to a meaty or fishy dinner, too fruity to be too rich.

A Plain Apple Tart

Serves 6–8
450g/1lb crisp, good-
  flavoured eating apples –
  Cox's, Granny Smiths,
  Golden Delicious
  or what you will
vanilla sugar
4–6 tbsp apricot jam

Make a pâte sucrée (page 140) with 120g/4oz flour, 60g/2oz unsalted butter, 2 tablespoons caster sugar and an egg. Chill, then roll out and line a 22cm/9 inch tart tin. Preheat the oven to 180°C/350°F/Gas 4.

Peel, core and quarter the apples, and spread over the pastry base in over-lapping, concentric circles, the circles also overlapping. Sprinkle vanilla sugar over the surface and bake for 45 minutes. Brush with warmed apricot jam that you have slackened with a tablespoon of water, but not sieved, and return the tart to the oven for 5 minutes. Equally good warm or cold.

Creamy Apple Tart

Serves 6–8
5 or 6 Cox's apples, peeled,
  cored and cut into 8
  segments
120g/4oz unsalted butter
180g/6oz vanilla sugar
300ml/10fl oz organic
  double cream
4 egg yolks
ground cinnamon or cloves,
  to taste

This creamy, caramelly tart is best made with a tarter eating apple such as Cox's. I think a whiff of musky-scented cinnamon enhances the flavour; you might prefer cloves.

Make a pâte sucrée (page 140) with 120g/4oz flour, 60g/2oz unsalted butter, 1 tablespoon icing sugar and 2 egg yolks. Chill, then roll out and line a 22cm/9 inch tart tin. Preheat the oven to 200°C/400°F/Gas 6.

Sauté the apple segments gently in the butter with half the sugar, until half cooked. Remove the apple pieces from the pan and let the sugar caramelize.

Mix together the cream, egg yolks, the remaining sugar and cinnamon or cloves. Place the cooled apples in tight circles in the pastry case. Pour first the caramel then the custard mixture over them, and bake for 35–40 minutes. Serve warm.

NORMANDY APPLE TART

Hot buttered apples, crusted with sugar, are all that is necessary for this deliciously simple tart, made with a crumbly, buttery, biscuity crust.

Serves 6 – 8
600g/1¼lb Cox's or other
   firm, sweet apples
60g/2oz unsalted butter
3 – 4 tbsp vanilla sugar, plus
   extra for sprinkling
beaten egg, for brushing
Calvados

Make a pâte sablée (page 141), chill, then roll out and line a 22cm/9 inch tart tin. Preheat the oven to 200°C/400°F/Gas 6.

Peel, core and thinly slice the apples. Cook them gently with the butter and vanilla sugar until golden and translucent, then leave to cool. Drain, reserving the juices.

Brush the uncooked pastry base with beaten egg. Place the apples – but not their juices – in concentric, overlapping circles on the pastry base and cook for 30 – 35 minutes.

Reheat the buttery juices, with a splosh of Calvados to enhance the Normandy connection, and pour over the tart with a sprinkling of sugar. Return to the oven for a couple of minutes; aim to serve it hot, when, in my opinion, it is at its best.

TARTE TATIN

The perfect autumnal or winter pudding: sticky, bittered caramel clinging to fragrant chunks of apple, and thick buttery pastry for the juices to seep into. With a melting lump of clotted cream this is consoling and warming food of the highest order. Don't let anyone deceive you into thinking it's difficult to flip the tart out of its pan. You just need to start with the right sort of pan. I use a heavy 25cm/10 inch diameter Cousances frying pan, with a short metal handle that goes in the oven. I also use shortcrust, although there are those who use puff pastry. Tarte Tatin was supposedly invented by the Tatin sisters at the Hotel Terminus Tatin near Orléans. History does not relate whether this famous tarte renversée was then made with other fruits in the way everyone does now, even using the principle for savoury tarts such as shallot Tatins.

Serves 8
90g/3oz vanilla caster sugar
60g/2oz unsalted butter
8–10 crisp, good-flavoured
   eating apples
juice of 1 lemon

Make shortcrust pastry (page 139) with 180g/6oz flour or use puff pastry (page 141), and chill while you prepare the apples. Preheat the oven to 180°C/350°F/Gas 4.

Put the sugar in the frying pan (see above) in a thin layer and heat it gently. Watch it all the time, as some bits will brown before others. You want the sugar to melt to a dark brown liquid all over without burning. On no account stir it, just shake the pan and turn it as you need to redistribute the sugar. Remove from the heat and immediately add tiny bits of butter, about a third of the 60g/2 oz, over the sugar. It will bubble instantly.

Peel and slice all the apples into quarters except one, which you should peel and cut in half. Core them all. Squeeze some lemon juice over them to prevent them from discolouring. Put a half apple, cut side up, in the middle of the pan, then a wheel of quarters around it, tightly packed. Dot with the remaining butter and place over a gentle heat to start it cooking. Remove from the heat.

Roll out the pastry to a circle just bigger than the frying pan. Roll it loosely over your rolling pin and thence use it to blanket the apples. Tuck the pastry down the sides of the pan like bedclothes to seal in all your apples, and bake in the middle of the oven for 25–30 minutes. Remove from the oven and leave to cool for 10 minutes. Cover the pan with a serving plate and flip the tart over on to it. Any stray fruit can be rearranged. The fruit should look glossily, gloopily burnished.

TARTE AUX POMMES

This is a half puréed, half sliced apple tart, made with cooking apples and enough vanilla to seep through the tart apple taste. This is best made with pâte sucrée, to heighten the sweet—sour divide.

Serves 6 – 8
900g/2lb cooking apples
180 – 200g/6 – 7oz vanilla
  sugar
1 vanilla pod, split lengthways

Preheat the oven to 200°C/400°F/Gas 6. Make a pâte sucrée (page 140) with 180g/6oz flour, 90g/3oz unsalted butter, 2 dessertspoons icing sugar and 2 egg yolks. Chill, then roll out and and line a 22cm/9 inch tart tin.

Peel, core and roughly chop half the apples, and stew them very gently with 120g/4oz of the sugar, the vanilla pod and its scraped-out seeds in a covered saucepan until almost puréed. You can then sieve them if you wish, or merely leave them to cool, depending on whether you prefer a coarsely textured or smooth result. Taste for sharpness, and stir in a bit more sugar if you have a wickedly sweet tooth.

When cold, fill the uncooked pastry case with your apple purée. Peel and slice the rest of the apples and arrange them as artistically as you feel moved to over the purée. Bake for 15 minutes, then sprinkle the surface with as much of the remaining sugar as you feel like and return to the oven until browned, about 20 minutes.

Hot, with cold pouring cream, this is wonderful, or you could bring a sophisticated note to what is essentially rustic food by making an airily light sabayon with some Calvados or cider.

APPLE GALETTE

Each region of Lorraine and Alsace has its own version of quiche, and the name is sometimes used for sweet custard tarts too. Old-fashioned Quiche Lorraine was made with a yeasted bread dough, and likewise the galette, a deliciously crisped, doughy crust harbouring a juice-sodden layer of apples, plums, greengages, apricots, or any of the scented fruits. You can scatter chopped nuts into the dough and over the fruit if you desire. This is not a dish that will good-temperedly reheat, it is to be eaten straight from the oven, or warm. However, you can keep the fruit and the rolled-out dough in the fridge, and finish off the pudding when you need it.

Serves 8

For the dough

200g/7oz strong white
   organic bread flour
2 tsp dried yeast
1½ tsp salt
2 eggs
5 tbsp melted unsalted
   butter
about 150ml/5fl oz water
   or milk at blood heat
a handful of chopped,
   toasted nuts – hazelnuts,
   almonds or walnuts
   (optional)

For the top

8 Cox's apples
150g/5oz unsalted butter
100g/3½oz vanilla sugar
   mixed with 1 tsp ground
   cinnamon and 1 tsp
   ground allspice (optional)
150ml/5fl oz double cream
1 egg
extra sugar
extra nuts (optional)

First, make the dough. Mix together the flour, yeast and salt, then add the eggs, butter and liquid to make a soft, coherent and unsticky dough. Knead by hand or in a food processor. Put the dough in a bowl inside a plastic bag and seal tightly; leave to double in size for at least an hour.

Turn out and punch down the dough, throwing in a handful of nuts if you feel like it. Lightly oil the bowl, roll the dough in it gently, and seal in a plastic bag for a second rise – 30 minutes should be enough this time. Punch down again and refrigerate; this dough will not roll out properly if it isn't chilled, it will shrink back temperamentally each time you attempt to roll it.

It should then be rolled out to about a 30cm/12 inch circle and placed on a well greased baking sheet or pizza plate.

Peel and core the apples and cut into wedges. Fry them in the butter until gently coloured, and then sprinkle them with the sugar and spice mixture. Let them begin to caramelize, then remove from the heat and cool to tepid.

If you are using plums or apricots, make a cut along the obvious division of the fruit and put about 700g/1½lb fruit and 180g/6oz sugar in a baking dish with a tablespoon of water. Bake until soft enough to extract the stones.

Preheat the oven to 200°C/400°F/Gas 6. Leaving 3cm/about 1 inch free at the edge, arrange the fruit and juices over the dough, put in a warm place for 20 minutes, then bake for 25 minutes.

Beat the cream, egg and a little sugar together and pour over as much of it as you can – the edge will have risen slightly. Scatter over the nuts if you are using them and cook until set, roughly 10 minutes.

APPLE CRUMBLE TART

A substantial tart, which you can make with puff or shortcrust pastry, the kind of pudding you would serve a team of post-match children, or hearty-appetited marrow-chilled grown-ups at a shoot lunch.

Serves 6
6 good, crisp eating apples
100g/3½oz unsalted butter,
    cut into small pieces
100g/3½oz flour
100g/3½oz nibbed almonds
150g/5oz vanilla sugar
a sprinkling of ground
    cinnamon or cloves
    (optional)

Preheat the oven to 190°C/375°F/Gas 5. Line a 22cm/9 inch tart tin with the pastry of your choice.

Peel, core and thinly slice the apples, and fill the pastry case with them. They will sink during cooking, so don't feel apprehensive if the base is high piled. Mix the remaining ingredients together quickly with your fingertips and pour the crumble over the apples, flattening it evenly by hand. Cook for 35–40 minutes: a skewer will tell you if the apples are cooked through, and the top should be beautifully browned. Serve with crème fraîche, clotted cream or crème crue.

KIRKHAM'S LANCASHIRE CHEESE AND APPLE TART

The perfect combination of deliciously lactic, crumbly Lancashire cheese with sweet, crisp eating apples, in a highly unusual tart: it can be served as successfully as a main course as it can as a pudding.

Caerphilly would do if you can't find the superb, traditionally made Lancashire; you want a crumbly lactic cheese with a fruity, acid flavour, not a melting, salty cheese.

Serves 6

60g/2oz unsalted butter

5 large Granny Smith's apples, peeled, cored and sliced

2 onions, thinly sliced

240g/8oz Kirkham's Lancashire cheese, coarsely grated

2 tsp fresh thyme leaves

salt and black pepper

1 small egg, beaten

Make shortcrust pastry (page 139) with 240g/8oz flour and 120g/4oz butter, adding a teaspoon of fresh thyme leaves to the mixture. Chill, then divide into two balls, one slightly larger than the other, and roll out thinly. Preheat the oven to 180°C/350°F/Gas 4.

Melt the butter in a heavy-bottomed frying pan, then add the apples and onions and cook gently until softened, 15–20 minutes. Remove from the heat and stir in the cheese, thyme and seasoning, then leave to cool.

Fit the larger layer of pastry into a 22–25cm/9–10 inch loose-bottomed tart tin or shallow pie plate, then heap on the filling. Cover with the top layer of pastry, seal and crimp the edges, and cut a cross in the middle for the steam to escape through. Brush with beaten egg and cook for 35–40 minutes. Serve warm.

Gooseberry Meringue Tart

Sharp and sugared, the tart gooseberry, like rhubarb, offsets the teeth-shocking sweetness of the light, crunchy meringue. When you tire of gooseberry fool, made with mashed gooseberries and thick home-made custard flavoured with elderflower, and of crumbles, pies and ice cream, this is a gorgeous midsummer pudding, made muscaty with elderflower.

Serves 6

22cm/9 inch shortcrust
  pastry case, chilled
  (page 139)
beaten egg white,
  for brushing
60g/2oz unsalted butter
2 tbsp light muscovado
  sugar
500g/about 1lb gooseberries,
  topped and tailed
1 tbsp elderflower cordial
  (Rock's is the best and
  is organic)
2 egg whites
1 egg yolk, beaten
60g/2oz vanilla caster sugar
1 tbsp plain flour, sifted
1 tbsp demerara sugar

Preheat the oven to 190°C/375°F/Gas 5. Bake the pastry blind for 15 minutes, then remove the beans, brush the pastry with beaten egg white, and cook for a further 5 minutes. Remove the pastry case from the oven and turn the heat down to 140°C/275°F/Gas 1.

Melt the butter in a saucepan, stir in the muscovado sugar and, when it is brown and bubbling, throw in the gooseberries. Cover with a lid and cook until they turn golden and translucent, shaking from time to time. Remove the pan from the heat and add the elderflower cordial. Leave to cool.

Whisk the egg whites until stiff, then gently fold in the beaten yolk, followed by the caster sugar and sifted flour, together. Fill the tart with the gooseberries, top with the meringue, sprinkle with demerara sugar and cook for about 40 minutes, until palely bronzed and cooked through. Serve warm, with thin pouring cream.

BAKED QUINCE TART

I planted my quince tree about ten years ago, and finally, three summers ago, saw the first couple of fuzzy-skinned golden quinces hanging bell-like from its branches. The following year there were half a dozen, last autumn a grand total of twenty. These golden apples attained mythical status for the Greeks; Paris gave one to Aphrodite, and they have become known as the fruit of love, of marriage, of fertility. The slightly bruised ones I bring indoors, their scent filling the autumn air with a promise of spring, of blossom with its heady sweetness. Mixed with apples or pears, the quince's rusty pinkness when cooked transforms its autumnal partners, as it does a soufflé, adding its unique granular texture too.

Turning straight to Jane Grigson's seminal Fruit Book *I came upon her 'Quinces baked in the French style'. I was captivated by the fact that a baked quince was Sir Isaac Newton's favourite pudding. I puréed the resulting dish, and set it inside a tart fragrant with Septembral mellow fruitfulness.*

Serves 6
22cm/9 inch shortcrust
  pastry case, chilled
  (page 139)
4 quinces
1 lemon
90g/3oz unsalted butter
120g/4oz caster sugar
2 tbsp double cream
4 tbsp demerara sugar
2 eggs, separated

Preheat the oven to 190°C/375°F/Gas 5.

Peel the quinces and hollow out the cores, not piercing the bottom of the fruit. This is a tedious and frustrating job, but I promise you it's worth it. Sprinkle with lemon juice as you go to arrest discolouration. Stand the quinces upright in a buttered gratin dish.

Cream together the butter, caster sugar and cream. Stuff the quinces with this mixture and top each quince with a tablespoon of demerara sugar. Bake until tender right the way through when pierced with a skewer.

If this is all too much for you, peel, core and chop the quinces into good-sized chunks, and cook them in a covered saucepan with the caster sugar and a little water until tender. Strain off the syrupy juice and purée the quinces with the butter and cream in a food processor. Taste for sweetness, then proceed as below.

Turn the oven up to 230°C/450°F/Gas 8. Purée the quinces in a food processor, then stir in the two egg yolks. Whisk the whites until stiff, fold them into the quince purée, then spoon the mixture into the uncooked pastry case. Cook for 15 minutes, then turn the heat down to 180°C/350°F/Gas 4 and cook for a further 20 minutes. Leave to cool for about 10 minutes before turning out and serving.

"Slightly bruised quinces I bring indoors,

their scent filling the autumn air with a promise of spring,

of blossom with its heady sweetness."

Vanilla and Raspberry Tart

I am writing this at the end of October, slightly disbelievingly. To be able to buy late-cropping Scottish raspberries when even the walnuts and quinces have been squirreled or brought down by the wind, and the last blackberries have vanished from the hedges, is a rare treat. It does not, however, feel quite right to serve them raw, as though it were the memory of a summer lunch. I had been thinking about inventing a vanilla tart, and this seemed the perfect late autumn combination. The sharp raspberries, unsugared, bleed a bit and rise to the surface, bright cerise dots that look like unblotted ink, slightly fuzzed into the brilliant yellow background of custard. Six egg yolks give it a powerful colour and flavour, with a predominant but not overpowering scent and flavour of vanilla. This is one hell of a rich tart.

Serves 6−8
300ml/10fl oz organic
   double cream
100ml/3½fl oz crème fraîche
about 200ml/7fl oz Jersey
   milk
1 vanilla pod, split
6 egg yolks
about 3 dsp vanilla sugar
1−2 tsp vanilla extract
300g/10oz raspberries

Preheat the oven to 180°C/350°F/Gas 4. Make a pâte sucrée (page 140) and chill, then roll out and line a 22cm/9 inch tart tin. Bake the pastry case blind for 10 minutes, then remove the beans, prick the base with a fork, brush lightly with beaten egg white, and return to the oven for 5 minutes.

Scald the creams and milk with the vanilla pod and its scraped-out insides. Put the egg yolks into a 900ml/1½ pint measuring jug and whisk in 2 dessert-spoons of the vanilla sugar. Add the vanilla extract, 1 teaspoon to start with. Whisk in the scalded creams, taste, and add more vanilla extract if necessary. I like mine strongly, but not overpoweringly, vanilla-ey. Add the last spoon of sugar if you think you need it.

Pull the tart case half out of the oven and shoot the raspberries on to it in a single, generous layer. Pour in the custard from the jug: this is the easiest, quickest way to decant liquid into a tart and ensure it carries on cooking, doesn't go soggy, and doesn't do the dreaded trick of seeping out of the pastry case and anointing the oven. Turn the oven down to 160°C/325°F/Gas 3 and bake for 40−50 minutes. Check after 40, and if set with a slight wobble, remove and leave to cool for 15−20 minutes. Turn out and eat warm.

ALMOND CREAM TARTS

Prune, cherry, greengage, plum, nectarine, peach or apricot, all are delicious sunk slightly into a gooey, almondy middle, laced with a splash of liqueur if you like, the fruit baked slowly in the oven first, yielding its sugary juices for you to jug and pour over the finished tart. Kirsch for cherries, Quetsche for plums, and last night I substituted Calvados for Armagnac, since I didn't have the latter, and thickly grated some peeled apple into the almond cream, which I covered in baked Agen prunes. The black-velvety fruit had first been soaked in a jar of prune juice. This was a perfect dish to follow chicken from the Westport Country Market, roasted with tarragon and lemon, and finished with cream, butter, the oniony pan juices, and more freshly chopped tarragon.

Serves 6—8

22cm/9 inch shortcrust
    pastry case, baked blind
    (pages 139–140)
about 24 prunes, soaked in
    water or prune juice to
    cover, or 15–18 apricots
    or greengages

Almond cream

120g/4oz ground almonds
100g/3½oz soft brown or
    vanilla caster sugar
100g/3½oz unsalted butter,
    melted
a few drops of Culpeper's
    bitter almond essence
1 large egg
2 tbsp double cream, or
    1 tbsp cream and
    1 tbsp alcohol

Whatever fruit you choose should be baked in a slow oven, with the liquid it has been soaked in if using prunes. For, say, greengages or plums, split the fruit, stone it, sprinkle it with sugar and add about 150ml/5fl oz of water. Bake until softened, then remove the fruit with a slotted spoon and pour the juice into a jug.

Preheat the oven to 220°C/425°F/Gas 7. For the almond cream, whisk together the ground almonds, sugar, melted butter, almond essence, egg and cream, plus the alcohol if you are using it. Spread the almond cream over the pastry base, arrange a layer of the baked fruit concentrically over the top, and bake until the cream has just set, 25—30 minutes.

You can glaze the tart if you feel like it, with apricot jam for green or golden fruit, and redcurrant for crimson, purple or black fruit.

ROAST FIG AND HONEY TART WITH COINTREAU

*This is a beauteous and sluttish, Fall of the Roman Empire kind of pudding. It looks
extravagant and decadent, and the taste of ripe black figs, honey and Cointreau is sweet and
pure, with the granular feel of the figs' innards to enhance the texture. Even if D H Lawrence
has rendered you unable to break open a fig without a degree of self-conscious caution,
you will be utterly seduced by this simple, sensual tart. Perfect for late summer and autumn,
a real painterly tart.*

Serves 6 – 8
about 15 figs
about 3 tbsp runny honey
   (use a good-quality honey,
   like Seggiano's chestnut
   honey)
30 – 60g/1 – 2oz unsalted
   butter, melted and
   warmed with 1 tbsp
   Cointreau

Preheat the oven to 200°C/400°F/Gas 6. Make shortcrust pastry (page 139)
with 120g/4oz flour and 60g/2oz unsalted butter, sweetened with 2 tablespoons
caster sugar. Chill, then roll out and line a 22cm/9 inch tart tin. Bake blind for
15 minutes. Remove the beans, prick the base with a fork, brush with beaten egg,
and return to the oven for a further 10 minutes.

Cut a cross half-way through each fig, squeeze gently and splay right open, then
fit them snugly together in the pastry case. Dribble in the honey, about ½ teaspoon
per fig (you could warm it slightly first to make it pour easily), then brush the
melted butter and Cointreau mixture liberally over the figs. Return to the oven
for 15 minutes. Remove from the oven and glaze the figs with the remainder of
the Cointreau mixture. Serve warm with crème fraîche with a touch of Cointreau
whisked into it.

Rhubarb and Lemon Cream Tart

A gaudily coloured pink and yellow tart, which is perfect for spring; sharp, fresh, with a dusting of icing sugar to add patches of brown when you blowtorch the top. I served this recently after a stickily delicious Osso Buco with its twin accompaniments of risotto Milanese and heavily garlic-spiked gremolata. I used a large tart case as I had ten to dinner, so adjust accordingly if you need to.

Serves 10
650g/1lb 6oz rhubarb,
    chopped into
    2–3cm/1 inch chunks
300g/10oz vanilla caster
    sugar
2 tbsp water

Lemon cream filling
1 egg and 6 egg yolks
120g/4oz vanilla caster sugar
grated zest and juice of
    1½ lemons
450–600ml/¾–1 pint
    double cream
the crumbs from a thick
    slice of Madeira cake, or
    60g/2oz boudoir biscuits,
    crumbled
icing sugar

Make a rich shortcrust pastry with 180g/6oz organic white flour and 90g/3oz unsalted butter, a generous tablespoon of unrefined sifted icing sugar, the grated zest of an organic lemon, and an egg. No water. Just swirl the lot together in a food processor until it coheres, then chill in cling film for an hour. Preheat the oven to 200°C/400°F/Gas 6. Line a greased 30cm/12 inch tart tin with the pastry and bake blind for 10 minutes, then remove the beans, prick the base with a fork, and bake for a further 5 minutes. Take out of the oven and leave to cool. Turn the oven down to 160°C/325°F/Gas 3.

Cook the rhubarb, sugar and water together slowly in a covered saucepan until the rhubarb is soft, then tip the contents of the pan into a sieve over a bowl and leave until the juice has finished dripping through. Reserve both separately.

For the lemon cream filling, beat the egg and yolks with the caster sugar, lemon zest and juice and the cream – the amount of cream you use will depend on the depth of your tart tin – then transfer to a jug. Put a layer of cake crumbs over the base of the pastry case and spoon the drained rhubarb on top of them. Put the tart on to a baking sheet in the oven and then pour the lemon mixture over. This means you do not have to carry a full, slopping tart to the oven. Bake until just set, about 25–30 minutes.

Sprinkle a thin film of icing sugar over the surface and blast it briefly with a blowtorch; alternatively, protect the pastry edges with strips of foil and put the tart under the grill. Cool, remove from the tin, and serve with a jug of the rhubarb juice and one of thin cream.

CORONATION DOUCET TART

I will never forget the first time I attempted the Coronation Doucet Tart. It had been served at Henry IV's coronation banquet, an elegant sweetener to the curlews, partridges, rabbits and small birds that made up the third course. When a great girlfriend, Anne, and I decided to throw a joint mediaeval birthday party, this honeyed, saffrony crocus-coloured tart was a must. We welcomed our guests in our scratchy, hessian, mediaeval maiden dresses, minstrels played in the gallery above, and a fanfare announced the triumphal arrival of the roasted wild boar, bedecked with bay and apple and supine on an old wooden door, as it was paraded before the diners. Each couple shared a wooden spoon, a pewter dish, and an invitation so authentic in its language and sealed appearance that one recipient was convinced it was a court summons. The monks, maidens, revellers, jesters, master and dancing bear then dug into the silky, creamy, soft-centred depths of the Doucet, with its mild yet intoxicating marriage of flavours. A taste from another age, yet the surprise of honey and saffron is somehow shockingly new, timely, brilliant with its clear notes of both sweet and intensely savoury.

Serves 6 – 8
22cm/9 inch shortcrust
   pastry case, chilled
   (page 139)
beaten egg, for brushing
325ml/12fl oz double cream
90ml/3fl oz Jersey or full
   fat milk
a good pinch of
   saffron threads
1 heaped tbsp runny honey,
   preferably lavender or
   chestnut
6 egg yolks

Preheat the oven to 190°C/375°F/Gas 5. Bake the pastry blind for 15 minutes, then remove the beans, prick the base with a fork, brush with beaten egg and return to the oven for 5 minutes. Turn the oven down to 180°C/350°F/Gas 4.

Gently bring the cream, milk, saffron and honey to scalding point. Take off the heat and allow the saffron to steep in the liquid, stirring it a bit to infuse the colour and flavour. Pour over the egg yolks and whisk together. You can pour the cream through a sieve, but I am happy to leave the saffron filaments in the finished tart, bleeding their brilliant orange into it. Taste, and add more honey if you need to. Pour into the pastry case and bake until set, but with a seismic shudder at its middle. Start checking after 30 minutes. Eat the tart warm.

You could serve it with some raspberries strewn with a little sugar and Kirsch alongside it in the summer, but I think you'll find you don't need cream, unless you are an addict.

RHUBARB, HONEY AND SAFFRON TART

Sharp, tart fruits seem to work best here, particularly, I suspect, because of the dominant flavour of honey when you compare it to sugar. Rhubarb, gooseberry or damson are all a sharp foil to the custard, and their sticky, syrupy juices can be poured warm over the top to offset the richness. You can lose the pastry altogether, and just make honeyed, fruited, saffrony custards, cooking them gently in little ramekins in the oven in a bain-marie.

If you are using damsons, don't attempt to stone them raw unless you are a complete masochist. Once cooked, use a cherry stoner, and don't worry about them not holding their shape, it's not the point of the pudding.

Serves 6 − 8
22cm/9 inch shortcrust
   pastry case, chilled
   (page 139)
beaten egg, for brushing
225g/8oz rhubarb, goose-
   berries or damsons
60g/2oz vanilla sugar
a piece of orange peel for the
   rhubarb; a head of fresh
   elderflowers or 1 tbsp
   elderflower cordial for
   gooseberries
a nut of butter
150ml/5fl oz water
325ml/12fl oz double cream
75ml/3fl oz Jersey milk
a good pinch of saffron
   threads
1 heaped tbsp runny honey
6 egg yolks

Preheat the oven to 190°C/375°F/Gas 5. Bake the pastry blind for 15 minutes, then remove the beans, prick the base with a fork, brush with beaten egg and return to the oven for 5 minutes. Remove the pastry case from the oven and turn the heat down to 180°C/350°F/Gas 4.

Meanwhile, stew the fruit gently in a covered saucepan together with the sugar, the orange or elderflower flavouring and the butter and water, until softened. Tip the contents of the pan into a sieve over a bowl, pick out the orange peel or elderflowers and leave until the juice has completely finished dripping through. Reserve both separately.

Gently bring the cream, milk, saffron and honey to scalding point. If the fruit is very sharp, add a bit more honey to the mixture. Take off the heat and allow the saffron to infuse for at least 15 minutes, giving it a gentle stir. Pour the saffron mixture over the egg yolks and whisk together.

Spread the fruit over the cooled pastry case, then pour in the custard and bake for about 30 minutes, until set with a shudder. Serve warm, with the juice in a little jug.

LEMON TART

This is the perfect pudding. I never tire of a state-of-the-art lemon tart. I have eaten and made scores of them, but this, for me, is the utopian version, with just the right sharp, gelled, rich creaminess. Just thinking about it is like putting sherbet on the tongue, instant salivation. I usually scorch the top with icing sugar and my blowtorch, but it is not mandatory. I like it hot, warm or cold, but I think warm wins by a whisker.

Serves 10

6 lemons

9 egg yolks – this is not
  a misprint!

325g/12oz vanilla caster
  sugar

300ml/10fl oz double cream

3 tbsp caster sugar
  for the top

Make a pâte sablée (page 141) with 240g/8oz plain flour, 180g/6oz unsalted butter, 75g/2½oz caster sugar and 2 egg yolks. Wrap in greaseproof paper and chill for an hour. Preheat the oven to 200°C/400°F/Gas 6. Roll out the pastry and line a 30cm/12 inch tart tin – there is something about a lemon tart that prohibits one from making it small. Bake blind for 10 minutes, then remove the beans and bake for a further 10 minutes.

Meanwhile, finely grate the zest of two of the lemons, then squeeze the juice of all six and set aside. Whisk together the egg yolks and vanilla sugar until thoroughly mixed. Add the lemon juice and zest and continue whisking, then whisk in the cream. Taste, and if it is not quite sweet enough, add a bit more sugar. Transfer the mixture to a jug.

As soon as the pastry is cooked, reduce the oven temperature to 120°C/250°F/ Gas ½. Pull the pastry case half out of the oven and pour the filling into it as high as you dare. Nudge it gently back into the oven and cook for about 30 minutes. The result should be barely set, wobbly and tremulous; it will go on firming up outside the oven. Remove and leave to cool for at least 20 minutes.

Scatter a thin layer of caster sugar over the surface and blowtorch it. If you haven't got one of these magical gadgets, protect the pastry with strips of silver foil and whack the tart under a hot grill until puddled with brown bubbles. Leave to cool slightly, even if you want to eat it hot.

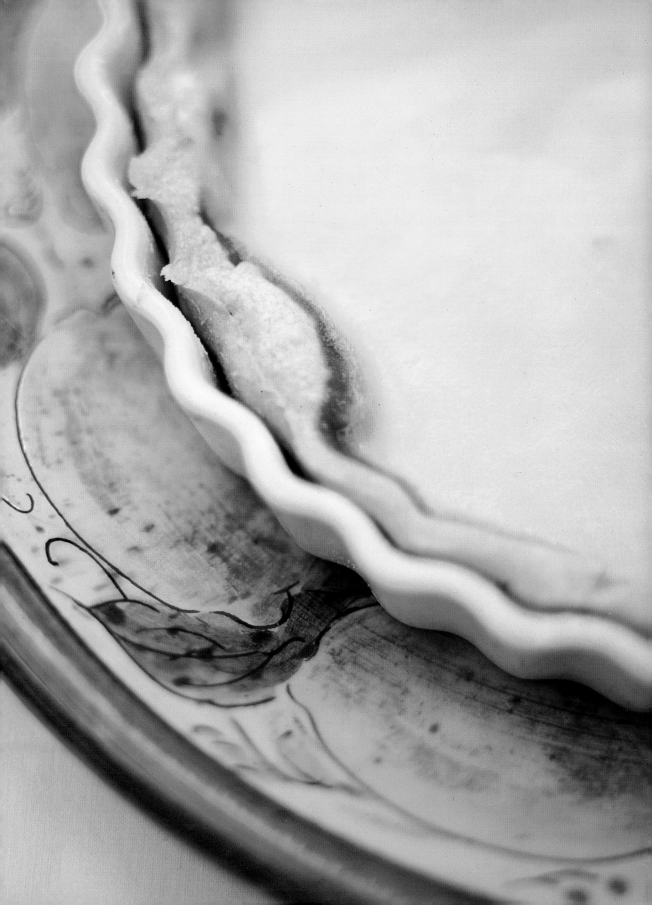

CHOCOLATE TART WITH PRALINÉED ALMONDS

This is a beautifully rich, chocolatey pudding, smart enough for a good dinner. A flourless and
pastryless tart, what a blessed relief — not that it is less rich than a more conventional tart.
It bursts into life with some really vanilla-ey ice cream to accompany it, the tart consumed at
room temperature with a dollop of cold alongside it.

Serves 10 – 12

120g/4oz almonds, skinned
   and chopped
1 tbsp unrefined icing sugar
150g/5oz best bitter
   chocolate
60g/2oz unsalted butter, cut
   into small pieces
60ml/2fl oz double cream
7 egg whites and 5 egg yolks
60g/2oz caster sugar
60g/2oz ground almonds
1 heaped tsp ground coffee
30g/1oz Green and Black's
   organic cocoa powder

For the top

150g/5oz best bitter
   chocolate
about 85ml/3fl oz milk

Put the chopped almonds in a gratin dish, throw the icing sugar over them and place under a hot grill, turning the dish every so often. You want the sugar to dissolve and adhere to the browning nuts. Watch carefully: brown, not black.

Preheat the oven to 180°C/350°F/Gas 4. Butter and flour a 30cm/12 inch tart tin.

Melt the chocolate in the top of a double boiler. Stir the butter into it, then stir in the cream and remove from the heat.

In a large bowl, whisk the egg whites with the caster sugar until stiff, then gently fold in the yolks, followed by the ground almonds, coffee and cocoa. Then fold in the chocolate, butter and cream mixture and mix gently to incorporate. Pour half the mixture into the tart tin, then add the pralinéed almonds to cover the surface, before pouring on the rest of the mixture. Cook for 15 minutes. Remove from the oven and leave to cool slightly before turning out on to a wire rack. Leave until completely cold.

For the top, melt the chocolate and milk together in a double boiler, then spread over the tart. When cool, you could gently sieve on a touch more cocoa, but don't be heavy handed; cocoa is bitter, with 70 per cent cocoa solids. I am anti the current trend of dredging everything in icing sugar, which is for sponge cakes as far as I'm concerned, or for brûléed tart tops.

PRUNE, ALMOND AND ARMAGNAC TART

Always try and find Agen prunes: good health food shops, delis and supermarkets stock them. Soak them in green gunpowder tea if you can, or smoky Lapsang Souchong as a second choice — it adds a subtly mysterious something to the end result. This is a classic trio, prune, almond and Armagnac, needing no excuses or tampering with.

Serves 6 — 8

22cm/9 inch shortcrust
   pastry case, chilled
   (page 139)
beaten egg, for brushing
4 tbsp double cream
2 eggs
120g/4oz vanilla caster sugar
120g/4oz ground almonds
4 tbsp Armagnac
1 tsp bitter almond essence
   (Culpeper's is good), or try
   orange flower water
60g/2oz butter
250g/8oz Agen prunes,
   soaked and stoned

Preheat the oven to 200°C/400°F/Gas 6. Bake the pastry blind for 10 minutes, then remove the beans, prick the base with a fork, brush with beaten egg and return to the oven for a further 10 minutes.

In a bowl, whisk together the cream, eggs, sugar, ground almonds, half the Armagnac and the almond essence or orange flower water. Melt the butter and whisk it into the mixture.

Dry the prunes on a paper towel and arrange on the pastry base. Pour the filling over them and bake for about 25 minutes. Sprinkle with the rest of the Armagnac, cool slightly and serve.

TREACLE TART

Gloopy, gooky, toothachingly sweet treacle tart, with a solid spoonful of clotted cream slipping deliquescent from the slice, turning buttery at the edges as it slides. The ultimate comfort food, to please die-hard traditionalist and the young and innocent-palated alike. This version has a softly gelled golden centre quite unlike the plain syrup and breadcrumb version, and once you have cooked it, you will no longer think what a cheek I've got for including a recipe for something that everyone knows. Or for telling you that when Julia Roberts comes to stay she drools over it, and busies herself making and twisting the pastry lattice for the top – which is how I usually serve it – all the quicker to cook it with. I associate her with this dish in the way one does when one knows one's friends' favourite dishes, and she deserves a mention every bit as much as the creators in the Other People's Tarts chapter.

I prefer a wholemeal crust for this tart, but please yourself. I find it lessens the impact of the rich sweetness, and a bit of bran is not a bad thing in the circumstances!

Serves 6 – 8
½ a large (900g) tin of
    golden syrup
30g/1oz unsalted butter,
    cut into small cubes
1 large egg, beaten
2–3 tbsp double cream
grated zest of 2 organic
    lemons
4 heaped tbsp brown
    breadcrumbs, preferably
    granary

Preheat the oven to 190°C/375°F/Gas 5. Make shortcrust pastry (page 139) with 120g/4oz plain or wholemeal flour, or 180g/6oz if you are going to add a lattice top. Line a 22cm/9 inch tart tin and chill. Bake blind for 15 minutes, then remove the beans, prick the base with a fork and bake for 5 more minutes. Turn the heat down to 180°C/350°F/Gas 4.

Warm the syrup gently, then, off the heat, add the butter and stir until melted in. Beat together the egg and cream and add to the syrup, with the lemon zest and breadcrumbs. Stir to mix evenly, then pour into the pastry case, add a lattice top if you like, and bake for 25–30 minutes. The filling will have set to a gel.

Leave for about 20–30 minutes before serving warm – there is nothing like hot treacle tart for taking the roof off your mouth. Dollop on some clotted cream, then go for a brisk artery-defying walk afterwards.

CUSTARD TART

I remember our local baker, known as 'Joan's Dad', used to make individual custard tarts in little foil cases when I was a child, with a speckledy sprinkling of nutmeg on the primrose surface. Every so often I was allowed 'out the back' of the bakery to see him skilfully fielding his wooden paddle into the bread oven to extract batches of loaves and cakes and pies, and the thrill of being offered a tart, a hot meat pie or an iced bun. I always chose the hot meat pie, with its crisp crust of lardy pastry and its hotly meaty, gravied interior. I have to confess, the custard tart is one of the few things I cannot, as a non milk drinker, bring myself to eat; although I can appreciate its silky, wobbly depths. It is just too milky for me. Perversely, crème pâtissière isn't. However, labour of love that it is, I recently made one for our wonderful nanny Gladys, who had looked after the children for nine happy years before her stroke last year. It has always been, like chocolate is for me, her weakness, her most special indulgence. And she knows a good custard tart when she sees one. It was not easy, knowing her to be an expert in the field, and that I'd have to smell the hot milk and contemplate the horror of the skin on top; so, this recipe has not been tested by me, but by an all-time custard tart fiend, who did not pronounce it wanting. When Gladys says something is 'all right,' you feel as though you've won the Olympics!

Serves 6 – 8
22cm/9 inch shortcrust
   pastry case, chilled
   (page 139)
beaten egg, for brushing
250ml/8fl oz Jersey milk
250ml/8fl oz single cream
2 little pieces of mace
½ a stick of cinnamon
2 large eggs and 2 egg yolks
60g/2oz vanilla sugar
1 dsp orange flower water
   (optional)
nutmeg

Preheat the oven to 190°C/375°F/Gas 5. Bake the pastry blind for 15 minutes. Remove the beans, prick the base with a fork, brush with beaten egg and return to the oven for 5 minutes. Remove from the oven and turn the heat down to 160°C/325°F/Gas 3.

Put the milk and cream into a saucepan with the mace and cinnamon and bring to scalding point. Beat the eggs, yolks and sugar together in a bowl and pour the hot cream and milk on to them, whisking as you go. Remove the mace and cinnamon, and add the orange flower water if you are using it. Pour the mixture into the pastry case and grate a suspicion of nutmeg over the top. Bake for about 40 minutes; it should be barely set with a faint tremor to it, as it will go on cooking outside the oven. I am reliably informed that it is best eaten warm. As long as I don't have to eat it, that's fine by me.

CHOCOLATE PECAN PIE

A good Sunday lunch pudding that children find moreish, particularly with a dollop of rich, vanilla-speckled ice cream on top.

Serves 6 – 8

22cm/9 inch shortcrust
    pastry case, chilled
    (page 139)
beaten egg white, for brushing
200g/7oz light muscovado
    sugar
300ml/10fl oz double cream
75g/2½oz best bitter
    chocolate, broken
    into pieces
2 egg yolks
a few drops of vanilla extract
120g/4oz pecan nuts,
    roughly chopped

Preheat the oven to 190°C/375°F/Gas 5. Bake the pastry blind for 15 minutes. Remove the beans, prick the base with a fork, brush with beaten egg white and return to the oven for 5 minutes. Remove from the oven and leave until cold.

In a double boiler, dissolve the sugar in the cream; before it is boiling, stir in the broken chocolate. Beat the egg yolks in gently with a balloon whisk, and carry on whisking until the mixture has thickened. Remove from the heat and stir in the vanilla extract and the nuts, then pour the mixture into the pastry case. Cool, then chill until set.

APRICOT TART

A glazed apricot tart with the tops of the fruit lusciously burnt, sharpness offset by sugar or crème pâtissière, is a great summer treat and beautiful to behold. I also favour this version, with the added bite of sour cream, and a sweetly syrupy glaze.

Serves 6 – 8

22cm/9 inch shortcrust
   pastry case, chilled
   (page 139)
beaten egg white,
   for brushing
about 17 or 18 apricots,
   halved and stoned
syrup made with 300g/10oz
   vanilla caster sugar and
   600ml/1 pint water
125ml/4fl oz sour cream
175ml/6fl oz double cream
2 eggs
caster sugar, to taste
60g/2oz unsalted butter

Preheat the oven to 200°C/400°F/Gas 6. Bake the pastry blind for 15 minutes, then remove the beans, prick the base with a fork, brush with beaten egg white and return to the oven for a further 5 minutes. Turn the heat up to 220°C/425°F/Gas 7.

Poach the apricots gently in the syrup until barely tender and still holding their shape. Drain and reserve the syrup. Beat the sour and double cream with the eggs, and sweeten to taste. Melt the butter and pour it straight into the cream mixture, stirring it in.

Place the apricots cut side up in the pastry case, starting at the edge and working in circles, slightly overlapping. Put the pastry case on the oven shelf, half out of the oven, then pour the custard in from a jug. Bake until tremblingly set and browned, about 20–25 minutes. Remove from the oven and leave to cool slightly.

Meanwhile, boil down the apricot poaching syrup to make a glaze, which you can brush on just before you are ready to eat the tart.

BAKEWELL TART

My grandmother's cook Rhoda never lost her touch at the stove, even after parting company with her memory. Unashamedly old-fashioned puddings and tarts – Bakewell, lemon meringue, treacle – appeared at the table alongside the Georgian silver cow creamers, the cream coming from my grandparents' farm.

Bakewell tart remains one of the great tastes of childhood. It is a recipe that should be left fearlessly alone, although that has become something daring, almost heretical, in these times of modern twists and fusions. To my mind, it should be considered just as modish to cook with conviction a dish that has fallen from culinary grace and bring it back into the fold.

Although Jane Grigson in her seminal English Food *assures us that only commercially made Bakewell tarts contain almonds, I think that, rather like the organic nature of the English language, certain things become absorbed into the culinary landscape to a point at which a new generation of cooks no longer questions their etymology.*

Serves 8

22cm/9 inch shortcrust
　pastry case, chilled
　(page 139)
180g/6oz really good
　raspberry jam; strawberry
　is good too
120g/4oz unsalted butter
120g/4oz vanilla sugar
120g/4oz ground almonds
4 egg yolks and 3 egg whites
1 tsp bitter almond essence
　(I use Culpeper's)
a handful of flaked almonds

Preheat the oven to 200°C/400°F/Gas 6. Spread a layer of the jam generously over the pastry base.

Melt the butter until it smells nutty. Whisk together the sugar, ground almonds, egg yolks and whites and almond essence, then pour the hot butter in and whisk to amalgamate. Pour this over the jam and bake until lightly browned and just set, about 30 minutes. After 25 minutes, strew the flaked almonds over the top of the tart, so they get a chance to brown slightly. A tart to be eaten 10 minutes after it comes out of the oven, still hot, with cold, thin cream poured over it.

Hazelnut and Apricot Tart

This is my variation on the classic Bakewell theme. If you can't be bothered with the Hunza apricots, just use the absolute best apricot jam, but the real thing does make a difference.

Serves 8

22cm/9 inch shortcrust
    pastry case, chilled
    (page 139)
225g/8oz Hunza apricots,
    soaked until soft in apple
    juice, then stewed,
    stoned and puréed
120g/4oz unsalted butter
4 egg yolks and 3 egg whites
90g/3oz vanilla sugar
120g/4oz ground hazelnuts
a few tbsp single cream
    (optional – see method)

Preheat the oven to 200°C/400°F/Gas 6. Spread the puréed apricots over the pastry base.

Melt the butter until it is golden brown. Beat the egg yolks and whites together with the sugar. Stir in the melted butter, then the ground hazelnuts. The mixture should be dropping consistency – if it doesn't feel quite slack enough you could whisk in a little single cream. Pour into the pastry case and bake for about 30 minutes, until the filling is set. Serve hot or warm.

Butterscotch Tart

I first ate this wonderfully melting, gooey tart at Old Head Hotel in the west of Ireland. Staying up to dinner was a novelty in itself, but this became one of the great childhood culinary memories, and remained so until I finally prised the recipe from the cook years later. The meringue was always put on to the top in sculpted serving spoonfuls, one per person, but we never stopped at one helping. How many hotels are there now where you can go back for more, indeed are encouraged to do so? I came up with a richer version than the original, using cream rather than milk, and darkly damp muscovado sugar, otherwise it's the same pudding we raved over 30 years ago.

Serves 6–7
22cm/9 inch shortcrust
   pastry case made with
   wholemeal flour, chilled
   (page 139)
beaten egg white, for brushing

Butterscotch filling
200g/7oz dark muscovado
   sugar
250ml/8fl oz single cream
90g/3oz butter
50g/scant 2oz cornflour,
   sifted
3 egg yolks
1 tsp vanilla extract

Meringue
3 egg whites
60g/2oz caster sugar

Preheat the oven to 190°C/375°F/Gas 5. Bake the pastry blind for 15 minutes, then remove the beans, prick the base with a fork, brush with beaten egg white and return to the oven for 10 minutes. Turn the heat down to 180°C/350°F/Gas 4.

Put all the ingredients for the filling in the top of a double boiler and whisk together over a low heat until thick, creamy and lump free. Then scrape the filling into the pastry case.

For the meringue, whisk the egg whites until stiff, add one-third of the caster sugar and whisk again. Add another third of the sugar and fold it in gently with a metal spoon. Either spread the meringue over the filling, or mould it into six or seven quenelle-shaped portions with two large spoons. Sprinkle the remaining sugar over the top and return to the oven for about 20 minutes, or until beautifully browned and crunchy on top.

CANADIAN PIE

Another winner from our childhood summers at Old Head Hotel in County Mayo. This was my father's and my brother Daniel's favourite, and I never managed to purloin the recipe from the cook, so after more error than trial, this is its closest approximation. Its honeyed, curranty sweetness is divine, not at all Christmassy, surprisingly enough, and perfect after a day facing the Atlantic breakers or climbing a mountain.

Serves 6

22cm/9 inch shortcrust
   pastry case, chilled
   (page 139)
beaten egg, for brushing
4 heaped tbsp golden syrup
1½ tbsp runny honey
30g/1oz unsalted butter
1 egg, beaten
2–3 tbsp double cream
150g/5oz currants
30g/1oz ground almonds
¼–½ tsp mixed spice
¼ tsp grated nutmeg
grated zest of 1 lemon
3 tsp lemon juice

Preheat the oven to 190°C/375°F/Gas 5. Bake the pastry blind for 15 minutes, then remove the beans, prick the base with a fork and brush with beaten egg, and return to the oven for 5 minutes.

Heat the golden syrup, honey and butter in a saucepan until liquid. Remove from the heat and stir in the beaten egg and the cream. Mix all the other filling ingredients together in a bowl, pour in the golden syrup mixture and stir well. Pour into the pastry case and cook for about 25 minutes, until nicely puffed up and browned. Serve with cream.

BLACK BOTTOM CREAM PIE

I came across this irresistible-sounding tart one blissful morning browsing in Kitchen Arts and Letters, Nach Waxman's wonderful cookbook shop in New York. Needless to say, it has its roots in the Deep South, and the legendary James Beard believed the first recipes for it were around the turn of the century. Its chocolate crumb crust is covered by a layer of darkly delicious chocolate pastry cream, signifying the black, swampy lowlands found along the Mississippi River. A froth of rum-flavoured chiffon tops this incontrovertibly old-fashioned pudding.

Serves 6 – 8

Chocolate pastry cream

4 egg yolks

6 tbsp unrefined sugar

4 tsp cornflour

500ml/16fl oz scalded milk

1 tbsp dark rum

1 vanilla pod, split

60g/2oz best bitter chocolate, broken into small pieces

Meringue chiffon topping

1½ tsp gelatine

100ml/3½fl oz double cream, whipped

2 tbsp dark rum

1 tsp vanilla extract

3 egg whites

6 tbsp unrefined icing sugar

½ tsp cream of tartar

Make a chocolate crumb crust in the same way as for the White Chocolate Tart with Raspberries (page 134), with 3 teaspoons (instead of 2) Green and Black's organic cocoa added to the pastry. Bake blind for 20 minutes, then remove the beans, prick the base with a fork, brush with beaten egg white and return to the oven for a further 10 minutes. Leave to cool.

For the chocolate pastry cream, whisk the yolks and sugar together thoroughly, until pale gold, then sift in the cornflour and blend until smooth. Whisk in the hot milk, then stir the mixture in a saucepan over a gentle heat until thickened. Add the rum and the scraped-out seeds of the vanilla pod, then add the broken chocolate and stir until melted and smooth. Scrape the chocolate cream into the pastry case.

For the topping, dissolve the gelatine in 2 tablespoons water, then add it to 1cm/½ inch of simmering water in a small saucepan and dissolve fully over a gentle heat for about 3 – 5 minutes. Stir into the whipped cream and blend thoroughly. Add the rum and vanilla extract, then cool over ice or briefly in the deep freeze, until the mixture is thickened, but not too cool.

For the meringue, whisk the egg whites until stiff, add one-third of the sugar and whisk again. Add another third of the sugar and the cream of tartar and whisk until glossy. Fold the remaining sugar in gently with a metal spoon, then fold the meringue into the gelatine mixture, and put on top of the tart. Refrigerate for a couple of hours if possible.

You can decorate with grated chocolate or cocoa powder if the spirit moves you. It is so sublimely rich, you might as well take it as far as you can!

WHITE CHOCOLATE TART WITH RASPBERRIES

I first cooked this tart at the end of October, when there was an unexpected and welcome supply of late Scottish raspberries. It made autumn recede temporarily, and then I couldn't resist cooking it again for a Boxing Day lunch party with my friend Brigid. We'd all been asked to bring a dish, and I happened upon some Third World flown-in berries, which it was worth abandoning seasonal principles for. I also took a Crème Brûlée Tart (page 136). White tarts are somehow fitting for Christmas food, particularly when they look like thick snow on top. I am not, on the whole, a flavoured pastry person, but Christmas brings on the aforementioned abandon, and a dark chocolatey crust made with Green and Black's organic cocoa is a delightful exception, and a contrast to the acre of white ice-rink topping it. Here, I dusted the top with cocoa at the last minute.

Serves 6 – 8

For the pastry

120g/4oz plain flour
2 tsp Green and Black's
   organic cocoa powder
1 heaped dsp unrefined
   icing sugar
60g/2oz cold butter, cut
   into small pieces
1 egg yolk

For the filling

200ml/7fl oz crème fraîche
250ml/8fl oz double cream
180g/6oz Green and Black's
   organic white chocolate
200g/7oz fresh raspberries

Preheat the oven to 200°C/400°F/Gas 6. Grease a 22cm/9 inch tart tin.

For the pastry, sift the flour, cocoa and sugar into the bowl of your food processor, add the cold butter and whizz briefly. Add the egg yolk and a tablespoon or two of ice-cold water, and process again just to the point at which the pastry coheres. Wrap in cling film and refrigerate for half an hour. Roll out on some flour sifted with a bit more cocoa and line the tart tin. Bake blind for 20 minutes, then remove the beans and cook for a further 10 minutes. The pastry case should be crisp and browned slightly. Leave to cool.

For the filling, heat the crème fraîche with 100ml/3½fl oz of the double cream. Break the chocolate into a bowl, pour the hot cream over it and leave for a minute, then stir until the chocolate dissolves. Cover with cling film with some air holes punched in it, and put in the fridge for 2–3 hours.

Very lightly crush the raspberries with a fork, just to let the juice run a little (they should remain whole), and put them in a single layer on the pastry base. Whisk the remaining double cream until thick but still soft, not rigid, and fold it into the chocolate mixture. Smooth this over the raspberry base with a rubber spatula and refrigerate for at least another hour. Eat cold.

CRÈME BRÛLÉE TART

As with the White Chocolate Tart with Raspberries on page 134, I made a dark cocoa crust for this tart. You can of course omit the cocoa and make a sweet shortcrust instead.

Serves 6 – 8

6 egg yolks

2 tbsp vanilla caster sugar

600ml/1 pint double cream

1 vanilla pod, split

3 – 4 tbsp unrefined icing
   sugar

Make a chocolate crumb crust in the same way as for the White Chocolate Tart with Raspberries (page 134). Leave to cool.

Whisk the egg yolks with the vanilla sugar, then continue to whisk in a double boiler, making sure the pan doesn't touch the boiling water, until the mixture has thickened and leaves a trail from the beaters.

Scald the cream with the vanilla pod and its scraped-out seeds in a saucepan, then whisk the cream into the egg and sugar mixture over the heat and stir with a wooden spoon until thickened, 5 – 7 minutes. Pour through a sieve into a bowl and leave to cool, then pour into the pastry case and refrigerate for 3 – 4 hours.

Sprinkle 1 – 2 tablespoons of the icing sugar over the surface and blowtorch until melted, or, protecting the pastry with strips of silver foil, place the tart under a hot grill. Sprinkle over the same amount of sugar again and continue until it is browned and bubbling. You will now have a glaze of caramel crackling. Put the tart in the fridge and chill for 20 – 30 minutes before serving.

CRANBERRY TART

The delight of a December fruit tart, scarlet and latticed, at the time of year when everything is dried, preserved and pickled, is distinctly elevating to the spirits, particularly a tart of such simplicity that you can knock it up when you are making cranberry sauce, one of the seriously satisfying parts of the culinary marathon. I always delight in the crimson berries popping like bubble-wrap or bladderwrack in the pan. At this time of year I often add ground nuts or grated orange or lemon zest to my pastry, although I am not normally given to this practice; in this case, almonds are best.

Serves 6 – 8
400g/14oz cranberries
1 orange
180g/6oz light muscovado sugar
200g/7oz mascarpone or cream cheese, sieved
1 small egg, beaten

Make a shortcrust-type pastry in the normal way (page 139), using 120g/4oz each of flour, almonds and butter. Chill, then roll out and line a 22cm/9 inch tart tin, and cut or pinking-shear strips of pastry for the lattice top. Chill the pastry case for at least 30 minutes. Preheat the oven to 190°C/375°F/Gas 5.

Put the cranberries in a saucepan and squeeze enough orange juice over them to almost cover. Simmer, uncovered, until the berries have all popped and you have a thickly bubbling red brew. Add most of the muscovado sugar, stirring it in and tasting for sweetness; add a little more if necessary.

Stir half the mixture into the mascarpone or cream cheese. Spread this over the pastry base, then cover with the remainder of the cranberry mixture. Decorate with the pastry lattice, brush with beaten egg, and bake for about 35 minutes. Best eaten warm.

MASTERING PASTRY

Just as the golden rule for house buying is location, location, location, so for pastry it is cold, cold, cold. Your butter should be chilled, your hands cold, and if you have a morgue-cold marble slab to roll the pastry out on, so much the better. I have even grated butter straight from the freezer when there has been none to be found in the fridge. Warmth and overworking are the enemy to the good, buttery-crisp pastry crust. I make my pastry in a food processor, and stop the button the moment the flour and butter have cohered into a ball, otherwise the results will be a cross between play dough and knicker elastic. Beware, but don't be frightened. Too wet or too dry, it can, like curdled mayonnaise, be rescued.

Shortcrust Pastry

The simplest pastry of all. I use 120g/4oz plain white (preferably organic) or wholemeal flour to 60g/2oz unsalted butter for my 22cm/9 inch tart tin, and 180g/6oz flour to 90g/3oz butter for a 30cm/12 inch tin. Rolled out thinly, these quantities fit perfectly. I would also use the smaller quantity for a 20cm/ 8 inch tin, in which case there will be a bit left over.

I sift the flour and a pinch of sea salt into the food processor, then cut the cold butter into small pieces on top of it. I process it for about 20–30 seconds, then add ice-cold water through the top, a tablespoon at a time – about 2–2½ should do it – with the machine running. If the paste is still in crumby little bits after a minute or two, add a tablespoon more of water, but remember, the more water you use, the more the pastry will shrink if you bake it blind. One solution is to use a bit of cream or egg yolk instead of water. The moment it has cohered into a single ball, stop, remove it, wrap it in cling film and put it in the fridge for at least 30 minutes.

If you are making pastry by hand, sift the flour into a large bowl with the salt, add the chopped butter, and work as briskly as you can to rub the fat into the flour, with the tips of your fingers only, rather like running grains of hot sand through your fingers. Add the water bit by bit as above; wrap and chill the pastry.

Then scatter a bit of flour on your work surface, roll your rolling pin in it, dust the palms of your hands, and start rolling. Always roll away from yourself, turning the pastry as you go, and keep the rolling pin and work surface floured to prevent sticking. Once it is rolled out, slip the rolling pin under the top third of the pastry,

and pick it up, judging where to lie it in the greased tin. Again, never stretch it, it will shrink back. Try to leave at least 30 minutes for the unbaked tart case to commune with the inside of your fridge. Or put it in the night before you need it.

Baking blind

If you are baking your pastry case blind, you will need to preheat the oven to 190–200°C/375–400°F/Gas 5–6. Some recipes also tell you to put a baking sheet in the oven to heat up. This can be invaluable if you are using a porcelain or other non-metal tart dish, as the hot baking sheet gives it an initial burst of heat to crisp up the bottom of the pastry. I know that some cooks will be shocked that I could even think of using anything other than metal but, as well as the aesthetic advantage when it comes to serving, china dishes are guaranteed never to discolour the pastry in the way that some metal ones do. If you are using a tart tin with a removable base (my preference, as they are by far the easiest to turn out), placing the tart tin on a baking sheet makes it easier to slide in and out of the oven.

Tear off a piece of greaseproof paper a little larger than the tart tin and place it over the pastry. Cover the paper with a layer of dried beans; the idea is to prevent the pastry from rising up in the oven. When the pastry is nearly cooked (the timing depends on the rest of the recipe), remove the paper and beans and prick the base of the pastry to let out trapped air that would otherwise bubble up. Return the tart to the oven for about 5–10 minutes to dry the pastry base.

Glazing

Brushing the partly baked pastry case with a light coating of beaten egg or egg white ensures a crisp finished tart

Pâte Sucrée

This pastry, enriched with egg yolks, is perfect for summer fruit and chocolate tarts. I normally make it like a standard shortcrust, with 120g/4oz flour to 60g/2oz unsalted butter, adding a tablespoon of sifted icing sugar and using 2 egg yolks instead of water. It is even more important to chill this pastry thoroughly.

Pâte sablée ('sandy pastry') is even sweeter, and crumbly, like a buttery biscuit. I use 180g/6oz flour to 120g/4oz butter, 60g/2oz icing sugar and 2 egg yolks. I put the butter, sugar and egg yolks into the food processor and work them together quickly, then blend in the sifted flour and work it into a paste. This needs longer chilling before rolling out, a minimum of an hour.

Puff Pastry

The richest, lightest leaves of buttery pastry, but it does take time, because of the resting time between each working of the dough. I refuse to compromise over the butter question: commercial brands made with inferior fats are just not what puff pastry is all about. As I have said earlier in the book, I often buy a 1kg/2¼lb sheet of it ready made and rolled from Baker & Spice (46 Walton Street, London SW3 1RB). It costs £16 and is well worth it, for the French flour, Lescure butter and the magic hands of their viennoiserie department.

180g/6oz plain flour
a pinch of salt
180g/6oz unsalted butter
about 150ml/5fl oz
    cold water

Sift the flour and salt into a mixing bowl, then rub in 25g/1oz of the butter, as for shortcrust pastry, or use a food processor. Mix in the water and then gently knead the dough on a floured surface, preferably marble. Wrap it in cling film and refrigerate for 30 minutes.

Keep the rest of the butter out to soften, then flatten it into a 3cm/1 inch thick rectangle. On a lightly floured surface, roll out the dough into a rectangle three times the length and 3cm/1 inch wider than the rectangle of butter. Place the butter in the centre of the pastry and then fold over the top and bottom of the pastry to cover the butter. With the rolling pin, press down on the edges to seal in the butter, then give the dough a quarter-turn clockwise. Now roll the dough out so that it returns to its original length. Fold over the ends again, press them together with the rolling pin, and give a further quarter-turn clockwise. Repeat the process once more, then rest the dough in the fridge for at least 30 minutes, remembering which way it is facing.

Repeat the rolling and turning process twice more, then refrigerate for a final 30 minutes before using or freezing. If the pastry gets warm and buttery at any stage during the process, put it in the fridge to chill.

INDEX

ACKNOWLEDGEMENTS

It is now the Year of the Dragon; it has just been the Year of the Tart. This is how it all began. I telephoned Agent George – Georgina Capel – who is always first in these matters, with the idea for the book. Her enthusiasm is legendary, if that is what she feels about the subject, and in this case, it was. She is not just the deal-maker, contract broker, high priestess of the proceedings, she is friend, cheerleader and adviser. As a non-obsessive cook, she is invaluable to the process. If she finds the writing of some of the recipes wanting, then she is right. I am, after all, writing for the 'home cook', a term which I take to mean everything from the keen and clueless to the off-duty professional. When I suggested to her that the cover might be off-putting to the 'keen but clueless' constituent, might look like unattainable restaurant food, she told me she'd immediately thought 'I could do that', and, better still, it had made her want to eat it instantly. So it stuck. Without George's support and enthusiasm, all things would be more difficult.

If you don't like the layout of this book, I imagine you are reading it because someone bought it for you. To me, the design is as integral to the look and feel of a good book as the text, and Lucy Holmes, who has designed this, and David Rowley the art director, have been instrumental in realising the full picture, and in making sure that the text and the look are so well married that they feel just right for one another. They have accomplished this to perfection.

Maggie Ramsay has had the onerous task of keeping me, my measurements, my textual shortcomings – and longcomings – under strict control. She has done this with constant good humour, precision, questioning and advice, for which I am hugely grateful.

Michael Dover, as publisher, is the man who can decide whether tarts fit into the overall scheme of things, whether they are a delicious, must-have addition to his list, or not; and luckily, in his wisdom, they were listworthy. I have yet to make him a tart, but now he can choose from *my* list, and he has a deal.

Susan Haynes is rather more difficult to categorise vis-à-vis this book, since she ended up playing rather more roles than she had bargained for. We had begun to get to know each other when we worked together on my last book, *West of Ireland Summers, A Cookbook*. This time, unfortunately for Susan, distance, in the shape of the Irish Sea, couldn't keep us apart. Once I'd decided to play home economist, and Susan had worked out my schedule, which included a manic eleven-tart day photographing material that was going to the Frankfurt Book Fair, it was quite clear to me, if not to her, that she would end up elbow deep in the Marigolds if I were to accomplish this ridiculously implausible feat. Without Susan, and my wonderful eldest daughter Miranda, an accomplished cook and sous chef at 17, eleven tarts in a day would have been whatever superlative you care to think of that goes further than impossible. It also goes to show how much more you learn about somebody in one day as part of your kitchen cabinet than you do after any amount of jolly lunches and meetings. Susan is someone whose temperature gauge remains, barometer-like, set fair, whatever the heat in the kitchen, and outside it, right through the last-minute uncertainties and problems that are bedfellows of the impending deadline. Thanks in Imperial measure.

The 'Other People's Tarts' chapter suggested itself very early on in the writing, not least because I looked to others for enlightenment and inspiration. I was also doing quite a lot of interviewing at the time, and it seemed crazy not to pick the culinary brains of the first-rate cooks I was writing about. And of the friends who just shared a passion for a really great tart. So I would like to thank all of you for your generosity in giving me such wonderful recipes.

David Loftus has an eye for light, composition, reportage, verité, and an elegance that is devoid of trickery and fuss. He is as sensitive a portrait photographer as he is with still lives. It is not as simple as it might appear to shoot a whole book of tarts, with each photograph original, different, true, and so earthily real that you feel you could eat the page. Without David, this book would not be beautiful.

The dedication is to my great friend Janie, whose friendship has been a constant for 21 years, and with whom I have shared most of the great pleasures of life: children, food, wine, films, books, theatre, music, Ireland, good conversation. In her inimitably unbossy, understated way, she is responsible for nudging me deeper into the profession of food writing than I would ever have dared to go. David and I took over her kitchen for the photographing of the book, the main memory of which is Janie returning every evening unfazed by the scene of casual devastation, the broken plates – the best one came from Divertimenti, who kindly lent me several beauties – and keener to sample that day's offerings than to have her kitchen back in its original shape and form. Her reaction, on being told that the book was being dedicated to her, was characteristic: 'I'm not quite sure what it says about me that the only book that's ever been dedicated to me is about tarts.'

It has been a real pleasure to work with all the talented people involved. I hope they enjoy the fruits – and savouries – of their labours.

Tamasin Day-Lewis